Sutton Coldfield
In The Forties

Sutton Coldfield
In The Forties

John Bassett

BREWIN BOOKS

First published by
Brewin Books Ltd, 56 Alcester Road,
Studley, Warwickshire B80 7LG in 2003

www.brewinbooks.com

ISBN 1 85858 201 6

A Cataloguing in Publication Record
for this title is available from the British Library.

Typeset in Times
Printed in Great Britain by
Warwick Printing Company Limited.

CONTENTS

ACKNOWLEDGEMENTS

I am most grateful for all the oral, written, illustrated and photographic contributions, plus the considerable amount of time people have invested in assisting me with the production of Sutton Coldfield in the Forties. The contributors are given credit in the text or captions.

Particular thanks go to my proof readers Jim Adler and Gordon Hudson, making sense of the Mss., Mrs Maureen Murray who typed some of the book, and my wife for her tolerance and for releasing me from some household duties.

The professional and valued support by Mrs Marion Baxter and colleagues of Sutton Coldfield Local Studies Library, the invaluable photographic input by Dr. John Raines and the patient help from the Brewin family and staff were all much appreciated.

Introduction

'SUTTON COLDFIELD IN THE FORTIES'

'Sutton Coldfield in the Forties', is a development of 'Cross City Connections' (1990) and 'Wheels Around Sutton, Lichfield and Tamworth' (1997) which combined data on public transport from local history perspectives.

This book includes events and developments in Sutton Coldfield from the 1930's to the town's awakening after World War II.

It is probable that this title and the next publication planned to deal with the 1950's, deal with the most eventful and significant twenty years in the town's long history. Additional material has been gleaned from copies of the 'Sutton Coldfield News' and various sources in the Reference and Local Studies sections of Sutton's Public Library.

The overall choice of material contains events and occasions that many Suttonians would acknowledge as of primary importance, though my particular slant, bias and balance will convey my own experiences of a working class person in a generally affluent Sutton Coldfield. Fortunately, contributions have come from many sections and locations within the town.

To my Warwickshire
born grandson Toby with love
from your Warwickshire
born grandad.

Chapter One

EMERGING FROM WORLD WAR II

We lived in a council house in Jerome Road, Sutton Coldfield, opposite the 1879 Midland Railway line. My World War II childhood memories include being frequently awoken in a frightened state during the nights by freight trains coming to a noisy, jolting, clanging halt, on the 1/100 gradient between Wylde Green Road and Sutton Park station.

Some residents in Ebrook Road, Jerome Road, Royal Road, Coleshill Road and Riland Road, were very anxious as the glow from the firebox was at times visible to enemy aircrew as they made their final approach to bomb munition factories and the Castle Bromwich airbase, in north Birmingham. In comparison with Birmingham, the bomb damage in Sutton was much less, though still very devastating.

The often poorly maintained steam locomotives that came to a halt close to our house were pulling long, heavy trains, well in excess of weight restrictions in peacetime. Generally the locomotive, having regained sufficient power, took part of the train to Sutton Park station, later calling back for the remainder, the train eventually being remarshalled and sent on its way at Sutton Park.

The location of the mobile artillery in the 1940s (Robert Paddison)

An Anchorage Road man recalled a special short train operated as required on the Park line, with a mounted gun on one of the vehicles. Apparently when the authorities were advised by Intelligence sources that German planes were on their way to follow the Park line through Sutton, Walmley, to north Birmingham, the train would stop in the cutting near Anchorage Road. Having secured the wagon with footings into the permanent way, bursts of fire were made at the German bombers passing overhead on their regular bombing sorties. To avoid detection, the train was swiftly moved away. It is not known how successful the train was, though it must have required some hastily amended timetabling on the Sutton Park and connecting lines. The severity of the cutting is shown in Robert Paddison's picture taken between Anchorage Road and High Street in the 1980's, during his professional railway duties.

No.5 BOMBER COMMAND, BIRMINGHAM NORTH!

Mr W. D. Sargent was one of 12 airmen evacuated from France in 1940 and then posted to No.5 Bomber Command, Birmingham North!

All the airmen were pleased to get a posting to another Bomber Command Centre, this time at Sutton Coldfield. The group arrived at New Street Station "very early in the morning and the kindly W.V.S. transported us in four private cars to Whitehouse Common in pitch dark. Our reaction in finding it was No.5 Balloon Centre was unprintable. Over the years there were only 3 left that stayed out of the 12". On reflection Mr Sargent "had a very pleasant period at No.5 Balloon Centre." The 1939 built depot had: 4 large hangars for Balloon repairs etc; living quarters for the R.A.F. and W.A.A.F; Parade Ground; large N.A.A.F.I; Administration Offices; Transport depot; Repair shops; etc. The main function of the No.5 B.C. Birmingham North was to maintain the Barrage Balloons in perfect condition for the defence of the City of Birmingham and the surrounding countryside.

Mr Sargent, at the time, a general duty airman, served on convoy duty bringing gas cylinders on large trailers from Runcorn to supply Balloon Squadron sites at Wythall, Yardley, Perry Park, as well as the Whitehouse H.Q. The No.5 B.C. base had anti-aircraft guns that were actually fired, though there is no confirmation of enemy aircraft being brought down on or near the site.

Despatch rider McCormack arrived at Whitehouse Common thinking he had been posted to a Bomber Command Centre, but seemed to adjust. He often escorted the transportation of gas cylinders to No.5 B.C. up to about 30 miles from Sutton. The Commanding Officer gave him a special mission in 1941 with the signed authorisation of a '658' permit to be on the roads in World War II. He waited on his B.S.A. 600 machine, 2 miles from Bassett's Pole on the Birmingham side of the junction. After a while an unidentified large black car arrived and then parked some distance behind him. A well dressed man in his 30's came from the vehicle, confirming firstly that the rider was from No.5 D.C. He then told the despatch rider to drive in front of the car to the Balloon Centre at 30 mph. This was to ensure that the V.I.P. would be on time for a base visit. The service personnel were aware that it was an important visit because they had to paint all the coal white!

The Inspecting Officer, H.R.H. The Princess Royal, nodded her head towards the honoured despatch rider, acknowledging his part in her safe arrival at No.5 Balloon Centre, North Birmingham H.Q.

A World War II Midland 'Red' bus timetable shows an intriguing service to No.5. There was a bus starting, not from Birmingham or Sutton Coldfield, but Wolverhampton (Queen's Square), as Service X15 to Whitehouse Common (Balloon Barrage Centre). Perhaps it was for servicemen and women arriving at Wolverhampton by train at the G.W.R. low level and L.M.S. high level stations. The R.A.F. may have thought it was less risky to bring personnel via Wolverhampton than Birmingham, also avoiding the half-mile walk between Snow Hill and New Street stations.

Later in the life of No.5 B.C, Mr McCormack remembered the R.A.F. men were reallocated to more appropriate tasks when W.A.A.F.'s personnel completely took over the careful maintenance and repairing of the Balloons. Apparently the women were more skilled, faster and suited to perform these jobs than the men!

LOCAL COMMUNITY ENTERTAINMENT

Gradually No.5 Balloon Centre activities ceased with the R.A.F. 216 M.U. working alongside the B.C. for a while. The staff of No.5 was taken over by the R.A.F. 216 M.U. in early 1942. Their parent unit was at Stafford. The Sutton camp remained virtually the same. Mr Sargent was promoted from Corporal to Sergeant. The M.U. "was again a large store supplying equipment, machinery, spare parts for the maintenance of fighter aircraft, etc., with existing staff retained".

With the blanket secrecy prevailing over service operations, it was not until the close of World War II that the wider public became aware that Spitfires were being tested and flown from Castle Bromwich Airfield by famous Test Pilot, Alec Henshaw. Yet, the less glamorous, but essential, supplying of equipment and stores to the routine and sharp end of R.A.F. activities remained the day to day workload of 216 M.U..

The civilian population of Sutton Coldfield regularly responded to the needs of service personnel, abroad and at home, by sending copies of the Sutton Coldfield News, parcels and letters constantly, demonstrating their love and support. Fortunately for residents in the Borough, the Officers and staff at 216 M.U. recognised and appreciated the sacrifices the local people made and encouraged morale through a regular programme of entertainment open to local people.

Open air Boxing - R.A.F. 216 M.U. - The C.O. and staff at the Whitehouse Common station opened up recreational events including boxing matches to Suttonians, to encourage public morale during W.W.II (W. D. Sargent)

At one outside event, a boxing ring was erected between the transport sheds and hangars. A programme of bouts was attended by Gus Lesnivich, Freddie Mills and Jack Solomons, who viewed the boxing programme with an excited and large appreciative audience of service personnel and civilians. Incidentally, one of the Unit's P.T. Instructors was Ned Tarleton, British and Commonwealth Featherweight Champion. Mr Sargent recalled that the "Great Bruce Woodcock - Heavyweight Champion, made his last amateur and first professional appearances at the Sutton Camp".

Most of the events were held indoors in the large entertainment room at the N.A.A.F.I. In the airmen's and airwomen's spare time they made toys which were then given away to Sutton children at the annual children's Christmas Party. Enthusiastically supported by the C.O, "the whole advertising and supply of display hoardings were supplied by my loyal gangs of workers", and himself, the Sergeant informed me.

The less known Gang Show - 'Ralph Reader's' first W.A.A.F. Gang Show was formed and performed at R.A.F. 216 M.U. (W. D. Sargent)

THE LESS KNOWN "GANG SHOW"

Later in this series, Ralph Reader will be mentioned in a world event at Sutton Coldfield in 1957, though an earlier show he initiated at 216 M.U. is less known. Mr Reader's 'Gang Shows' were very popular in the Scout Movement, but he formed and had performed the first 'W.A.A.F. Gang Show' on the Sutton base. Sgt. Sargent made the entertainer aware of the acting and singing abilities of two Sutton W.A.A.F.s. After the required auditions and discussions, the two Warwickshire Servicewomen became Gang Show members, performing regularly at Sutton.

Mr Sargent was also responsible for widening the entertainment experience of a 90 year old Christian woman. The base C.O. with the Sergeant, arranged for the Mother Superior of the Sutton Convent, where the C.O.'s children were educated, to see and hear her first 'talkie film'.

Did the occupants of Whitehouse Farm's cottage know the building was in German Photographic records? (Birmingham Library Services)

GERMAN VIEW OF NO.5 BALLOON CENTRE

Martin Collins sent an interesting picture that demonstrated the Germans were very much aware of No.5 Balloon Centre at the beginning of World War II and presumably planned to avoid the balloons' attendant anti-aircraft batteries.

The Luftwaffe's aerial picture, on 21 October 1939, clearly shows Bedford Road, coming off Rectory Road, the junction of Rectory Road, Whitehouse Common Road and Hollyfield Road. The word 'Sutton Coldfield' is shown just behind the Boot Inn. There is a heavily drawn line or a fence around the Balloon Centre, stretching from the rear houses on the east side of Whitehouse Common Road, behind Withyhill Road, Lindridge Road and back down Rectory Road, towards the junction on the brow of that road. On the west side of Bedford Road is the present Good Hope Hospital site.

Mrs Sigrid Mustow translated "that it was a secret picture, part of a wartime survey including the Barrage Balloon Centre, Sutton Coldfield, where special troops were based".

The Luftwaffe's aerial view of No.5 Balloon Centre in October 1939. (Martin Collins)

FIRST BASE POST OFFICE

Another Borough Military location was the American Army Post Office which opened in the Sutton Park L.M.S. Goods shed on 1 July 1942. Martin and Frances Collins in 'Letters for Victory' (Brewin Books 1993) share the memories of G.Is and Suttonians. Martin informed me that the main Post Office buildings opened in October 1942, closing in November-December 1945.

In addition to accommodation in local homes, the Upper Holland Road School, later called Riland-Bedford, and Plantsbrook was also used from 30 June 1942 until it was de-requisitioned in May 1945. The Nissen huts at the Streetly camp opened

Sutton Park with postal sorting facilities, used by American and British service people. (M. Lewis)

in 1944, closing in 1945, amongst other Sutton area sites. What the Collins describe as a "terrible loss" on 12 April 1945 was the death of President Franklin D. Roosevelt. He was also the Commander-in-Chief of the U.S Military forces. An American flag was flown at half mast over Sutton Town Hall on Sunday 15 April. The day was set aside for mourning. The Collins continued "Impressive services were held in the Congregational and Holy Trinity Churches, with all detachments attending". The deep relationships made between Suttonians and the American forces personnel did make it a day of mourning for many in Sutton Coldfield.

WORLD WAR II - SUTTON PARK REFRESHMENTS

Present day readers of World War II life in Sutton could be excused for thinking that little happened apart from service activities in the Borough. However local people made the effort to maintain some normality. Mrs Lilian Hunt, wife of chimney sweep Tom serving abroad in the Army, was one lady who comes to mind. She used ice cream powder, ice, etc. from Birmingham, serving home made ice cream to customers from a kiosk at Wyndley Pool. She continued doing this from 1937-1966.

In World War II, wood was gathered to make a fire, surrounded by bricks, with iron bars to support the iron waterpots and kettles. Mrs Hunt told me "We served cups, pots or jugs of tea, prices ranging from 2d. per cup to 1/- or 2/- per pot or jug depending on size. A full tea of bread and butter, jam, cake and tea cost 1/-". When the kiosk was at the bottom on Palace Hill, they were near the wooden Bandstand. A different band played there every Sunday night in the season. There were military bands playing. She also recalls the "visits by Amington Silver Band".

Mrs Hunt said "Farmers used to buy the soot collected by Tom on his chimney sweeping rounds, as soot is an excellent fertiliser, particularly for growing potatoes". At one point "in the War", Lilian commented "Sutton Council bought all the soot that was available to sprinkle on Wyndley Pool, because it was thought that the German pilots were using the Pool as a flightpath on the way to bomb Birmingham".

Well known Sutton Chimney Sweep, Tom Hunt and wife Lilian, pre W.W.II.

During German day attacks, the pilots may have noted the Crystal Palace amusement park and miniature railway were operating at some Wartime holiday periods.

FUNCTIONAL TO LUXURY AIR RAID SHELTERS

Mr & Mrs Steventon's Coles Lane air raid shelter was in the house. It had a "steel top with wire cage round it". This was known as the "Morrison" shelter. Thinking of gas masks, the worst thing "was the one for baby, having to practise putting her in. Having to carry masks was a bind but we got used to it". Alerted by the air raid siren, another family trooped out to their shelter one dark night. As the members stepped inside there was panic and shouting as they walked into a shelter floor covered with ice cold water that had seeped in from a previous rain storm.

For my younger brother David and myself, our council garden Anderson shelter was made cosy and comfortable by Mother. Our emergency visits during World

War II to the shelter seemed more an adventure, with our loving, protective parents assisting when we came face to face with spiders, beetles and all manner of creepy crawlies. With the deep earth covering of the shelter, we used it in later years as a little hill to run up and over it.

In Patricia Price's poem about World War II, she recalls:
"The young ones often tell me I'm living in the past,
But one day they too will know that days fly much too fast.
And in memories times of yesteryear seem just like yesterday,
For we were there before the days of plastic and the pill,
And those who caught us scrumping were 'Coppers', not 'The Bill'.
'Sheltered housing' was the place when air raids caught us hopping,
Dad had made to keep up safe whilst Hitler's bombs were dropping".

Mrs Margaret Wood's father was a Chartered Electrical Engineer, building the family a "superb air raid shelter that one could sleep in." He copied the design of an ocean liner cabin "for the Walmley Road shelter". In previous years he had sailed to New Zealand. This is where the idea of cabin bunk beds probably originated.

Arthur Wilkins in Jerome Road, remembered that the family "had an Anderson shelter in the back garden". His Dad had made a cement interior to try to keep it dry. There were bunks and we often slept in there all night". He recalled "air raid drill at Victoria Road Boys' School, sitting in the arches under the school". Arthur described Headmaster, Mr Gregory "as very strict", whereas the "History Teacher, Mr Bromwich, was a kind old gentleman". Pamela, with her parents, James and Doris Baker, the licencees of the Fox Inn, Walmley, shared the Anderson shelter of the village greengrocers, Mr & Mrs Wood, in the "latter part of the War as our cellar was deemed unsafe owing to many getting trapped underground as a result of the bombing".

Arthur Adderley "was quite surprised at my Mother being so upset at the beginning of World War II, though she had gone through it before". According to the 'Dandy' and the 'Beano' he remembered, "that we would win the War by Christmas 1939". "We had several bombs around Jockey Road. One night, one exploded outside a garage, narrowly missing a petrol tank. We thought our house would have been destroyed but we were overjoyed when we came outside the shelter to find the window frames and the walls of the house still intact. The reflection of the moon made it look as if all the glass had been blown in. The sewage and gas pipes were ruptured and sewage came in and flooded the back gardens."

Arthur also recalled "we had about eighty bombs in and around Sutton Coldfield Park. Some German P.O.W.s rebuilt a wall around Keepers Pool".

Richard Shrive's grandfather was an A.R.P. Warden in the town "under the Empress Cinema" he advised me. "There was a Searchlight Unit stationed in an

James and Doris Baker with daughter Pamela, in Walmley. (Mrs P. D. Done)

adjoining field to Princess Alice Orphanage. German bombers used to jettison their bombs and make off as fast as they could" commented Miss Janet Nixon. That meant the Orphanage had a "lot of broken windows. Fortunately there were no casualties, except poor Bonnie, the farm horse".

Mr & Mrs Steventon remembered "A wooden hut was erected at the rear of the South Parade Slipper baths, as a mortuary, and baths facilities themselves to be used for cleansing and rinsing in case of gas attacks".

David Owen, OBE, Chairman of Rubery Own Holdings Ltd. advised that "my father had an air raid shelter. We dug one under the lawn at 'The Highway' where Mr A. G. B. Owen and his wife lived after they married in 1932". David had memories of the shelter as "very cold and damp and let in water". His father then had the garage at 'The Highway' close to New Hall, converted into a form of bunker with very thick walls, "which we used most of the time".

As a toddler in Victoria Road, Jeanette can recall "When the sirens went, mom would put us in the big pram downstairs in the hall, out of the front door, around the side of the house, then down the sloping long garden into the Empress Cinema car park." From there they went in the shelter under the Empress.

TROOP TRAIN "LIFT"

L.M.S. main line driver Loveridge of Aston shed was familiar with "Germans bombing" railway installations, freight services and when the Luftwaffe had "the tip off", troop trains were targets. His son wrote "Dad was driving a troop train from the north of England to somewhere south and was stopped at Crewe". The driver, who for a time in post-war years drove New Street/Four Oaks locals (because of speeding on the mainline), was amazed, but delighted, to have one of the U.K's leading railway executives come to the loco's cab. Before they departed Sir William Stanier spoke to Dad and told him that he had to attend a "very important meeting" in Birmingham. Their train was going non-stop, so "Dad would have to be certain to stop in Brum!" His son continued, "which of course he did, with 20 minutes to spare". William Stanier came to the cab and thanked them. He gave them £5 each - a lot of money in those days, for a train crew. Stanier House, in Holliday Street, Birmingham, was named after Sir William Stanier, who was Chief Mechanical Engineer of the LMS Railway, 1932-1944.

INNOCENT CASUALTIES OF WAR

Wars bring pain, sorrow and death to many individual and vulnerable children in all countries in time of war for both victors and losers. The Princess Alice Orphanage in New Oscott, Sutton Coldfield (part of the National Children's Home) cared for children who needed love and security, whether without parents or a parent, for the remainder of their lives or for a certain period of time. Janet Nixon, a dedicated care worker at P.A.O. from 1936 -1978 told me "we never referred to the children as orphanage children".

Olive wrote saying "I have recently received a copy of my records for the time I was at P.A.O.: 1942 -1950 and they had 6 monthly reports which included any ailments which we had over the years we were there. Nursing care was very good. I remember I was very young, wearing an all-in-one night suit - fluffy, with feet. I remember being frightened to go downstairs on my own, in case I slipped, but there was always someone to help me".

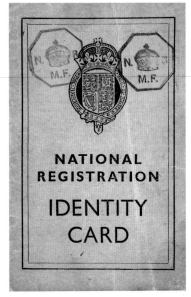

The Front cover of a National Registration Identity Card. (Alan Smith)

Olive continued "there were about 12 houses for girls and the same for boys. These were separated by a huge grassed play area which is now a Tesco supermarket. We were cared for very well. There was a House Matron plus an assistant. The number of children in each house was about 12. It was just like living in a large family. We had a games room and we slept in dormitories.

"At Christmas time we all had two huge piles of presents, one to be opened in the morning and the other after dinner. Mr Lenton was the man in charge of the Orphanage. Our House Matron we referred to as 'Auntie'".

FIRST BABIES' HOSPITAL

Princess Alice's Orphanage remains fairly well known around Sutton, but another facility for children that closed near the Royal Town's border in 1953 is far less known. Ask about Canwell Show and a good proportion of Suttonians have visited it or read about the actual event in the local papers. Canwell Baby Hospital, the first in the U.K. and opened in 1931, was accommodated within Canwell Hall.

Susie King was the Night Superintendent in 1938 -1953. She recalls "It was the first specialist hospital for babies, part of a national plan for regional provision throughout the United Kingdom". Canwell was primarily for the Birmingham conurbation but accepted babies from Tamworth, Sutton Coldfield and other towns. Although Canwell Hall was in the Lichfield Rural District Council area, Sutton Coldfield was the nearest town with the greatest population, so its postal address was written as "Near Sutton Coldfield".

Canwell initially cared for babies from birth to 5 years. Before and during the war years, babies were still considered to be babies up to 5 years of age. No comparison with modern babies! The 6 main wards cared for a total of one hundred babies, with a variety of contagious or infectious diseases. The T.B. Balcony followed the current practice of an open-air treatment area, which brought good results, when the disease was caught in its early stages.

Canwell Hall Baby Hospital - Night Superintendent - Susie King.
(Susie King Collection)

Miss Harris nursed there from 1942 -1947, with the hospital being run by the City of Birmingham for the care of sick children aged from birth - 5 years. Miss Harris stated "that the children came from some of the poorer parts of Birmingham."

Canwell people saw the babies being pushed around Canwell Hall, often two, three and four in a pram. The nurses were well known to the locals and so great interest and concern was shown in the progress of the sick children and their welfare. Mr Rubery knew Jimmy Stainthorp was a stoker at the Hospital. Apparently the equipment produced gas for the hospital's heating and cooking needs. The Canwell villagers joined the nurses for dances.

My father earned a low wage as a cowman. Basic foods like milk, eggs, vegetables and occasionally bacon and meat supplemented the wage, providing the family with a reasonable supply of produce. From Jerome Road, 5 year olds came within the catchment area of Duke Street Infants School, where I started my education in the early years of World War II. I was inconsolable at being parted from mother. I carried on crying even when placed on the rocking horse. So I was taken off the horse, never being invited to have a further ride - much to my disgust in later years! There are vivid memories of Cadbury's chocolate biscuits and little bottles of milk. I hated milk, loving chocolate biscuits instead. Overall the time spent at Duke Street was a happy one.

I cannot remember having school meals but Dr. Harper looking back to the later years of the war wrote, "I went to Green Lanes Infant School... getting splinters from sitting on wood block floors with the constant smell of disinfectant. Consequently, being sick was not uncommon. School meals, which I did not have, were horrendous. They came in large metal containers - by lorry from a central kitchen - resembling mostly a greasy slurry of fatty bits of meat, swimming in an oily gravy. Also there were smaller containers of stringy cabbage and other strange vegetables".

My father digging for victory in Jerome Road. (Author)

SOUTH PARADE BRITISH RESTAURANT

Did those metal containers come from South Parade? Mayor, Councillor W. Moss, opened the 200 seater British Restaurant in Wesley Hall in February 1943. It could serve 500 lunches, plus 700 school children's lunches (also prepared in the kitchen). It had been estimated that up to that time, only 5% of Sutton's population could be catered for in its catering establishments at lunchtime.

From personal knowledge, if the British Restaurant did supply Green Lanes Infant School, then I can inform Dr. Harper, the meals I had there were good and wholesome. Sometimes "surplus to requirement portions" arrived in our house, for my father! Some years later my mother was a food server in the Restaurant.

Arthur Adderley "remembered the rationing very clearly". If someone you knew was walking down the road, they would tell you they had got 'such and such' a food at a certain place. So you would run back and tell your mum and she "goes to try to get some."

PIONEER MOBILE TAKEAWAYS

If there is a Guinness British Record for the first mobile takeaway service, a Suttonian may have been able to make a justified claim. Mr Pyatt informed me of one Ted Flanagan at 47 Riland Road who in World War II "had opened a Fish and

Pioneer Takeaway Service - Ted Flanagan was probably one of the earliest pioneers of mobile fish and chip services from his Riland road premises. (Bernard R. Haynes)

Chip shop about 200 yards away from the Power Station. At this time he used to go around the area with his trailer loaded with chips, etc. When he was on Home Guard duties at the Coleshill railway bridge, he used to nip up to his shop and bring us free fish and chips. His shop was busy serving the R.A.F. lads from the Balloon Barrage Station about a mile away in Rectory Road on their way back to Barracks late at night." Mr Pyatt remembered that local lads and girls "went to the dances there."

It seems when "Ted had any electrical trouble at his premises, he used to walk down to the Electricity Station and get whoever was on emergency call to go up to his place and sort it out". If the duty electrician was Harry, they had a bottle of beer in the back room shop and he would give me a pile of fish and chips to come back with to my depot". Mrs Hunt noted "Mr Flanagan used to tour around the Sutton Public Houses on Saturday nights. I can remember buying fish and chips from his trailer outside the Cup Inn. I think it cost about 1s 2d".

Sutton Coldfield local history photographer, Dr. J Raines found he "got a lot of chips for 6d". Thinking of Ted's pioneering work, the doctor recounted "Mr Flanagan used to sell fish and chips in the evening to people coming out of the Dog Inn and the Empress Cinema from a low, cream-coloured metal trailer attached to his car. This was also used at other times to take fish and chips to the R.A.F. base in Rectory Road".

RAILWAY PIONEERING WOMEN

World War II brought to the fore the untapped employment resources, abilities and potential women offered, when their menfolk were in the Forces. This was in addition to the repairing of balloons! Miss Eileen Kirkham, 23 years old, of Stonnall was the London Midland and Scottish Railway Company's (L.M.S.) first signal woman, taking a post at Sutton Park Signal Box on the busy freight,troop and hospital train route in the Spring of 1942. It was not long before Miss Kirkham was joined by Joan Price and Louise Hall, so the 3 day shifts, 6am-2pm, 2pm-10pm and 10pm-6am were covered by signalwomen.

Mrs Price found that "some older railwaymen discriminated against the women for taking signalling positions". Joan advised me that if a 'red alert' bombing raid warning in the night was received from Saltley, the duty signalwoman/man rang the platform bell to alert the fire watchers from the goods department. Permanent wayman Walter Roberts, from the Sutton Coldfield (L.N.W.R.) P.W. gang told me "our ganger impressed upon us that under no circumstances, when we were on night firewatching duties at Sutton Park station, should we go into that box when a woman was on duty".

Mrs Price informed me that "troop trains were regular users of that route. The signalling staff had to give those trains priority, so they carefully listened for the engine whistle codes indicating which routes they needed at the Park Lane or Walsall ends".

During the war, the bombing of Curzon Street and Lawley Street goods depots, near the centre of Birmingham, resulted in the admin. staff from the two centres being accommodated in the Sutton Park station up and downside buildings. In the booklet celebrating the opening of the reconstruction of the L.M.S. Lawley Street Goods Depot on 29 October 1945, mention is made "of a fire in 1937 and damage which was sustained by enemy action during the War".

David Wiseman wrote that "during the War, clerical and invoicing staff were evacuated from the Goods Offices at Central, Curzon Street, Lawley Street and Landor Street to Sutton Park station as a precautionary measure, to take as many people out of central Birmingham as possible". David spoke of relocated staff being accommodated in the "Sutton Park

Women to the Rescue - Mrs Joan Price was one of three women the L.M.S. recruited to staff the Sutton Park signal box during 1942-45. (Author)

Goods yard in rail coaches and prefab buildings", though Joan Price and Charlie Curtis have no recollections. The significance of the transferred depot's work in the War was seen by a dining car being moved to Sutton Park station and placed behind the signal box to provide meals for them. Charlie Curtis remembers food waste from the dining car put into a skip in a refuse truck. The crimson dining car soon became a dirty colour. On moonlight nights Mrs Price often saw "the rats playing on and around the railway lines". On other occasions she "could hear the rats playing on the signal chairs underneath the box". The signal woman also recalled "In the War years, there were not many fitters about so the engines were in bad condition, with as much weight put behind them as the officers thought could be pulled".

ROYAL SLUMBERS

Prior to Signalman Charlie Curtis moving to the Nuneaton area for the 3 signalwomen to staff the Park box, similar to Mr McCormack, he has a royal story to tell. In February 1942, King George VI and Queen Elizabeth, later known to us as the Queen Mother, demonstrated their loyal support to Midland people in the War, by visiting Birmingham, Coventry, Nuneaton and Sutton. The Royal Train was parked overnight in the Sutton Park freight siding. Charlie was on nights. In an effort to ensure the Royal couple could enjoy an undisturbed night's sleep in the reasonably quiet location, train drivers coming through Sutton Park were prohibited during that night to blow their whistles, advising the signalling staff which routes they wanted on reaching the Walsall or Park Lane junctions, as Mrs Price recounted.

We are not sure if the Wellingborough to Bescot freight driver could not read his special notice or if he was anti-royal, whatever, but he gave long penetrating whistles as he approached the small compact box, blacked out as required. Shortly afterwards Charlie took a phone call from railway control about the incident, presumably alerted by either police, railway officials or Royal train staff.

Royal Signalman Charlie Curtis. An irate Saltley Controller rang Charlie when the occupied Royal train was in Sutton Park freight sidings. (Author)

An angry voice responded to Charlie's "Sutton Park Box", with "put the Inspector on". In those war years, even more protection was provided for Royal Family members, so a signalling/traffic inspector was on Royal duty with the signalman. My being intrigued by the outcome, Mr Curtis told me "the Inspector was asked by control if he had heard the illegal engine whistling. The resident box inspector said "no" and put the Internal railway telephone down". Probably wrongly, I suggested the Inspector was telling a lie. Charlie said "Certainly not, he was truthful. When the whistle was being blown he was sound asleep". Charlie smiled, "Control never asked if I had heard the whistle!"

LOCAL 'HOPS'

In addition to dancing at the R.A.F. Camp and occasionally at Canwell Hall the "main venues in Sutton were the very popular Maney Church Hall and the more up-market Crystal Palace in Sutton Park (subsequently re-named The Orange Grove)" according to Mrs Patricia Price. At Crystal Palace "professionals Sid Perkins and Edna Duffield often gracefully demonstrated just how we should be dancing our quicksteps and waltzes". The more proficient danced the rumba, the tango and the foxtrot. However "we were all able to join in with great gusto for the Palais Glide and the Lambeth Walk."

During the interval in the ladies' room the girls, having been suitably revived with tea or fizzy lemonade, "discussed the merits of their respective partners and applied another layer of Coty face powder to flushed cheeks and shiny noses". Speculation focused on, "which of their favoured partners they would be dancing with for the last waltz when the band played "Who's taking you home tonight?"

Not surprisingly local girls had noticed the opening of the American Army Post Office and the personnel who worked there. Thinking about dancing crazes, Mrs Price can remember the American 'invasion' of Sutton Coldfield "bringing the G.I.s with their own particular styles of dance - the energetic jitter-bug, rock and roll, jive and the smooching dances where one rarely moved from the spot!" Those routines became accepted in time and "often included in the programme by public demand as the sound of The Glen Miller Orchestra became the music of the day".

ATMOSPHERIC SHOP

There was an almost addictive quality about the aroma from a Station Street shop for train passengers walking or scurrying past to catch Birmingham services in World

The Station Street Atmospheric Shop - Mr M. Shaw's, Saddler and Harness Maker Shop had tantalizing leather aromas for customers and railway passengers. Misses Cynthia and Thelma Shaw rest on the shop steps, C. 1930. (Misses Shaw)

War II. The fine wooden name board above the shop, close to the Congregational Church hall proudly pronounced 'H. Shaw, Saddler and Harness Maker'.

One of Harry's five daughters, Pamela, recalled "having been born and bred at the combined house and shop, family members did not notice the smell of the different leathers, so potent to customers and passing railway passengers". Mr Shaw had owned the business for 50 years and was a familiar businessman going to Sutton Coldfield area farms, to measure horses for their particular collars. Tackle was repaired for Evans, the butcher on the Parade, and Mr Shaw sold horse nosebags, accessories for dogs, a selection of fine leather luggage, handbags, wallets and fishing tackle. Cynthia informed me with pride that the "Station Street business was also a sports outfitters". The workshop in the rear looked on to the Congregational Church. Of the five daughters, three daughters, Frances, Cynthia and Gladys, worked as saddlers.

SWEET TOOTH CELEBRITIES

Another shop that fascinated me was in High Street, across from the Three Tuns. Just after the War, where with umpteen other children, some accompanied by parents, we waited with our pocket money and ration coupons for the family allocation of confectionery. Betty Robbins had worked in the shop before World War II when it was owned by Elsie Richards. She sold it to Mr Rudder in 1940, a sweet factory proprietor.

According to Betty, some Birmingham Theatre managements, seeking to protect their leading artists from the city bombing raids, arranged accommodation for them in the Three Tuns. Some of the stars that came across the road included Ivor Novello, who Betty described "as a regular customer", Muriel Barron and "Richard Tauber, who came in more than once".

During World War II, the shop "opened for a couple of hours in the morning and perhaps one hour after lunch. The stock coming from Mr Rudder's factory included kali suckers, blocks of toffee, wrapped chocolate, bottled sweets and lollipops. Queuing was orderly, although one could wait a long time".

Betty was called to work on munitions at the I.C.I., Perry Barr, between 1943 - 45. She served me amongst hundreds of others from 1945. To parents and children in 1945 "6d", she reminded me "was a lot of money in those days".

PUBLIC TRANSPORT ADAPTATIONS

Ethel Burton remembered the Government "commandeered" A. T. Hastilow's "Tudor Rose" coaches of Park Road and "the one my husband Syd drove went down at Dunkirk". In World War II she added "Hastilow staff went anywhere they were wanted on removal work. Two drivers would go and accommodation was paid for, if necessary, when spending one or two nights away from home".

The local Midland 'Red' suspended services in the June 1940 timetable were: X12, Birmingham via Sutton to Lichfield, Burton, Derby; 172, Sutton-Coventry, S61, Sutton-Wishaw; and S62/3, Sutton - Chester Road. The workman's Sunday return was 1/-. between Birmingham and Sutton.

In June 1944, Sutton to New Street trains left at: 6.25, 7.50, 8.50, (all a.m.) 12.10, 12.25 sx, 12.42 so, 1.06, 2.15, 4.18 so, 4.45 sx, 5.15, 5.35, 6.00, 6.45, 7.23, 9.30, 10.52, (all p.m.).

(so: Saturdays only, sx: Saturdays excepted).

Even with the heavy use of troop, hospital and freight services on the Midland line route, a meagre number of five passenger trains remained in 1944 from New Street, Birmingham to Walsall, via Sutton Park.

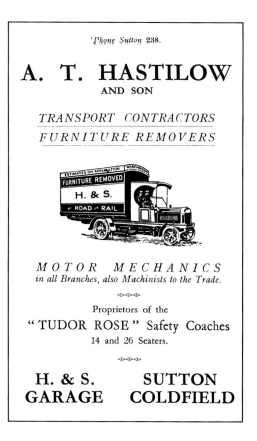

An Hastilow, Park Road, advert in a 1935 publication.

BUSINESS CASUALTIES

Similar to the bombing of the railway goods offices at Curzon Street and Lawley Street, a menswear business in the City Arcade, Birmingham, which had expanded to 3 units was destroyed in a single night by German bombing in 1941. So J. W. Hicks moved into the former premises of Meeson confectioners at 91 The Parade.

John Hicks, the grandson and son of the two proprietors, informed me "that they were confronted with the monumental task of keeping the business running as all their stock had been destroyed in the Blitz. I think the strain proved too much for my grandfather since he died a fortnight after the move was made. This left my father in sole charge." John's father was found physically unfit for military service.

"Due to my father's prudence", John continued, "the business survived the War after which my uncle returned from military service to rejoin the firm".

Woodcock's shop on the Parade was a newsagents and stationers. In the War all the windows were blacked out. The owner's sister and uncle ran the shop. The uncle acted as treasurer and book-keeper. The company also operated a printing business, with further shops at Tamworth and Kingston-on-Thames. Mr K. J. Woodcock worked in management at the Sutton Coldfield Highways Department Depot in Riland Road before serving in the R.A.F..

SUTTON LAUNDRY LTD. - MAJOR EMPLOYERS

Kate Gardiner's picture of a Sutton Laundry Ltd. horse and van provoked a considerable amount of research and interest. Marian Baxter traced from the Sutton Coldfield Library Local Studies resources that the Laundry was established shortly before the first World War. The premises included a fifty foot chimney near the main building. However, the O.S. map for 1938 shows the chimney in a different position from the area originally occupied by the stables, harness room and cart shed at the rear of the site. The 17, Coleshill Road address occupied most of the area between the Brass Foundry (Martineau Works) and the road now known as Broomie Close. Dr. John Raines sent in a 1937 advertisement, noting the Laundry services available at the time.

Kate Gardiner's grandfather, Herbert Maeer, worked for the Sutton Laundry in the 30's and 40's. "The cart with horse in South Parade in Kate's photograph, includes grandad, two other local children and herself on the right. As she points out the cart was fitted with the more recently introduced rubber tyres.

Branley McDonald was a laundry van driver, similar to Mr Hall, Norman

A 1937 advertisement of services offered by The Sutton Laundry Ltd (Dr. John Raines)

Herbert Maeer in South Parade with his horse and van showing granddaughter Kate (right) and two other local children. (Kate Gardiner)

Driver John Morrall with Sutton Laundry's first electric van. (Edna Morrall)

John Morrall's elder brother, Dick with assistant Albert in Bedford Road. (Edna Morrall)

Hassall and Tom Harris. From memory he recalled the horse drivers in the inter-war years were "Mr Maeer, Jack Showell, Tom Carrington and Sam Hipkiss." Branley thought the horse in Mr Maeer's picture was "Dolly, who had to be put down, and replaced with an electric battery operated vehicle." With Mr. Hall, Branley took two Bedford vans to an army camp in Aldershot, advised by the M.O.T. Commander "there would be a hot meal there for them." I was informed "when we got there the Cook sergeant laughed. he gave us a cup of tea, a cheese sandwich and a railway travel warrant."

They arrived at Birmingham at 2a.m. and there was no public transport. He gained a lift to Gravelly Hill, walking the remaining journey to Reddicap Hill.

Pat Townsend, née Morrall, a near neighbour in Jerome Road, informed me that her uncle John worked at the Laundry until it closed at Easter 1960."

Another Jerome Road teenager was Daisy Dolphin, working at Sutton Laundry in 1944-46. "The washing was brought in by horse and cart, later by vans", she mainly remembered the horse and carts. Daisy worked on the calendar machine. "The ladies sorted the washing into big containers, and the men operated the washing equipment."

CLANDESTINE MILITARY CORRESPONDENCE

Daisy, now Pierce, said that in the war years she was employed in a separate section dealing with service people's washing. It was not unknown for the women to "find notes from soldiers at the Packington camp. There was an open invitation to the monthly camp dance." Daisy recalled "a lot of girls from laundry went to the dances", perhaps from a personal invite!

Doris Smith and sister Edna recalled that the Sutton Laundry was a major employer in the town, particularly for women. Their picture taken at the Laundry on Trinity Monday, 1938 includes many of the female staff, with some of the girls, dressed up on the company's float, taking part in the day's procession which attracted participation from the majority of Sutton's firms and businesses. Although it was a holiday, the laundry workers, worked. The 1937 float emphasized England's continued commitment against further hostilities in the Laundry's theme of 'Peace to all nations.' The processions began at King Edward square travelling

Some of the large contingent of Sutton Laundry staff with colleagues dressing up for the Whit Monday 1938 procession. (Edna Morrall / Albert C. Aston)

The Sutton Laundry's 1937 Trinity Monday float emphasized the U.K.'s commitment against another world war. (Edna Morrall)

via the Parade to Rectory Park. One of the regular entertainers at the Town's special days, including Trinity Monday was Jim Phillips who dressed up as a clown, using a pig's bladder like a balloon to entertain the children. He obtained them from Evans' the Butcher. His relatives said "He raised a lot of money for charities."

CHARIOT OF FIRE

The Royal Sutton Laundry moved its dry cleaning facilities from King Edward Square to Coleshill Road, enabling an expansion of its services to industry, commerce, forces, hotels, catering and the general public. It became known as the Sutton Laundry Ltd.

A further photograph of Edna Morrall recorded a 1947 visit to the laundry by the Mayor and Mayoress, with the Mayoress receiving a bouquet from Miss Alford, the youngest employee at the laundry at the time. To the right of the Mayor is Mr Charles Smith, the laundry manager. Behind Miss Alford is Mrs Hildred Sinclaire-Ford, a director. The Ford's Dry Cleaners and Dyers incorporated into The Sutton Laundry Ltd, was named after Mrs Ford, whose husband had been another

A 1947 visit by the mayor and mayoress to the Sutton Laundry Ltd, meeting staff and directors, including Mr Frank Cattell, on the right. (Edna Morrall)

director. On the extreme right is Mr Frank Cattell. According to Mrs Edna Morrall, Mr Parkes sold the Falcon Lodge area to Mr Cattell, who subsequently sold it to the Sutton Council for the development of the model municipal housing development. Mr Cattell was my father's employer. Edna described Frank Cattell "as a Gentleman Farmer. He later moved to Wentworth Road in his retirement."

Amongst the Laundry management Doris and Edna remembered: "Miss Nellie Bull was an Office Manager, Mr Brown was the wash-house foreman, Miss Hettie Price ran the packing department, with Mrs Yapp being in charge of the Calendar, where items were ironed." The sisters described the Calendar as "ten times bigger than a normal size mangle."

An unnamed manager, representing the Laundry in a Sutton procession, took his part as a Centurion very seriously, dressing up correctly in his role. The manager discussed the need for two horses to pull the chariot with Arthur Smith, the father of Doris and Edna. In the early 1930's the laundry had around forty horses, which were rested on a regular basis at Holland House, the later site for the Riland-

Bedford School. Mr Smith suggested Dolly or Betty, the two staid workhorses. Going against expert's advice the manager selected two fine black horses to pull the chariot. As the chariot set off in the procession, many were complimentary of the turnout of the vehicle and the Centurion. All went well from the Council House, along the High Street, but going down Mill Street, the brass band burst into life, with much bell ringing. Suddenly the fine chariot horses hearing the bells reverted to their paramount duties of pulling a fire tender, hurtling down the remainder of Mill Street, along the Parade, with the Centurion manager holding on to the chariot to avoid being thrown out amongst procession floats and the delighted public. A very embarrassed and weak kneed manager was relieved when the horses came to a stop in Wylde Green, with their substitute fire appliance.

TWO COLOUR FRIENDSHIP

Some of the Laundry girls considered the R.A.F. approach to them was more subtle than the soldiers. Rather than risk the non-arrival of notes in trouser and shirt pockets, the Castle Bromwich R.A.F. wrote messages on the end of the washing list attached to the garments. It certainly worked for Joan. She later married Harold, moving with him back to Kidderminster.

Laundry staff in front of the Coleshill Road offices. The windows are protected against war damage. The office staff are not known. The two people in the back row (in overalls) are Mrs R. Jones and D. Lamb. The front row ladies in overalls are Doris Smith, W. Payne and I. McDonald. (Edna Morrall)

The W.A.A.F. based at the Holland House, Upper Holland Road had their washing collected direct from Coleshill Road Laundry. One of the American women asked Edna "why she was not wearing nail polish?" The local girl told the servicewomen, "It cannot be brought in this country". The next time the american collected the washing, a delighted Edna received two complimentary small bottles of different coloured nail varnish.

At an evening get-together between American Forces personnel at the Penns Lane camp and the Sutton Laundry girls, the guests had "nice size slices of a plain cake with jam in it and a rich thick cream on top." Although Edna really enjoyed the butter made cake and cream, it unfortunately made her violently sick!

Chapter Two

1945 – THE EVENTUAL VICTORY

The Sutton Coldfield News, like other media sources had been restricted in its reporting under the Defence of the Realm Regulations Act from the beginning of hostilities on 3 September 1939. Many Suttonians obviously knew about No.5 Balloon Depot, the First Base Post Office and military activities in Sutton Park and P.O.Ws in the area.

EYES AND EARS OPEN

Folk still kept their eyes and ears open as they enjoyed the Park, with information known about the Civil Defence Camp near Powell's Pool and the first testing ground for amphibious tanks at an old brickyard pool. An unofficial military move, probably not made public before now was told me by Arthur Adderley. "My oldest brother was in the Tank Regiment. One day I came home from school and lo and behold he had driven a tank out of the convoy down Chester Road, turned down Jockey Road and left his tank in a side road. He came in the house to have a cup of tea with our widowed Mother!"

In July 1945, the Parks and Estates Committee heard Metro Cammel Carriage and Wagon Co.Ltd. anticipated closure of the tank testing facilities. Debate moved on to levelling the ground and possible afforestation of the area.

Six months earlier, the belief in the hoped-for end to the war was becoming more likely. However, the N.A.A.F.I. still actively advertised for women to serve as 'Miss Naffys'. They were of great help on leave trains, serving drinks and snacks, in special buffet trains providing much needed refreshments for service men and women on the move in the U.K. Theatre goers were offered "The Dancing Years" with Ivor Novello at the Birmingham Hippodrome. Tessie O'Shea, Bruce Carfax and Billy Danvers were appearing in "Red Riding Hood" in the Theatre Royal, New Street, Birmingham.

The exceptionally cold weather over Christmas 1944 brought heavy demands on the rationed coal supplies, with mines already working reduced output.

It was noted in February that the Borough Restaurant received excellent ministry reports on its methods of food preparation and the quality of its meals. Manageress Mrs Morgan announced the "financial results were very satisfactory".

WARTIME JOY RIDERS

Continuing co-operation in the services was in evidence by the R.A.F. 216 M.U. Band playing at a Home Guard Association Dance; admission was 7/6. Vacancies advertised in the local paper included "Headmaster required for small mixed school, salary £175 p.a. increasing by annual increments of £25." Alternatively a "Housekeeper was required for £3 weekly in a comfortable, Four Oaks home." Modern readers may be surprised to find that joy riding is not exclusively a late 20th century phenomenon. Four Kingstanding boys raced off in an unlocked car from the drive of a friend in Hardwicke Road, Streetly. The car was found abandoned miles away.

George Rose's best King Edwards potatoes cost eight shillings per cwt, carrots were five shillings and sixpence for ½ cwt, and swedes were five shillings per cwt.

On 24 March the Rev. John Hickey Boggon was inducted as the 44th Rector of Sutton Coldfield. The Bishop of Birmingham in the 'call' spoke out against the "effect of falling moral standards".

There was much concern in 1945 that Sutton Coldfield Council's Education Committee authority was passed over to Warwickshire County Council under the Education Act of that year. Suttonians also worried that local rates increased by two shillings and twopence for County purposes. Local politicians pointed out "one quarter only of local taxation was controlled by Sutton Borough Council".

VICTORY CELEBRATIONS

The Sutton Coldfield News of May 12 1945 announced "Victory bells ring out in a new Europe" with the major war effort coming to an end. On V.E. Day evening, dancing went on until the late hours in King Edward Square against the twenty-two ensigns of the United Nations and the carefully decorated Council House. There was standing room only at the Service of Thanksgiving on Sunday 13th May in the Parish Church in which English and American servicemen and women participated with Home Support Organisations.

The Adderley family "were overjoyed when the war ended. Sutton celebrated in great style and we had the Bands come out in the Parade. Ronny Hancock's was the local band. He played and we all had a good time - well into the morning".

Victory parties amongst many others were reported in Riland Grove with a late evening dance including R.A.F. 216 M.U. guests, Highbridge Road, Park Hill, Windyridge Road, 3 roads sharing Little Aston Parish Hall. The children's party in Jerome Road was a new experience to most of us, with tables full of goodies set up in the road. The adults had worked extremely hard, some making sacrifices from limited provisions.

V.E. Day, King Edward Square - The flags of the allied nations at Sutton Town Hall. (Martin Collins)

A rousing welcome was given by relatives and friends to returning local Prisoners of War in Bracebridge Cafe. Mrs F. W. Terry, the Mayoress, presided, supported by other Council members. During the rally it was announced that thirty eight local men had either been repatriated, escaped or liberated. Even after eight months' of peace, the results of war were still very much in evidence. Sutton people were advised that their Ration Books were obtainable from the Town Hall, Boldmere Road, Mere Green Shopping Centre, Fox Hollies Road, with a personal touch from Mrs E. K. Dyer, J.P. for Minworth applicants.

A mammoth party for 600 wounded service personnel, including many shot down over Germany, was held in July at the Crystal Palace in Sutton Park. Music was provided by the Teddy Thomas Orchestra. There were table tennis exhibitions and amusements for the children all being free. There were many distinguished guests present at all these festivities.

HOSPITAL PROVISION INADEQUATE

The expected arrival of thousands of demobbed servicemen and women into the Borough caused anxieties and problems for local hospital providers. The daily average of in-patients and out-patients in 1943 was twenty-three, rising to forty-two in 1944. Good Hope Annexe cared for twelve resident patients in its first 9 months. Alarm bells also rang over the long list of patients waiting for hospital treatment. Who should be given priority? Our courageous lads and girls back from abroad or the local people who sacrificed such a lot in the last 6 years? The obvious need was to increase hospital provision quickly and provide a Maternity Unit - surely, many folk argued, there will be a baby boom soon! It was not difficult to assess and predict need with the anticipated growth in population, but where were the resources to adequately meet those needs to come from?

Officer Caley was billeted with the Smith family during his posting with the American Postal Service at Sutton Park Station, becoming an accepted member of the Sutton household! (Alan Smith)

The most negative emotion that began to grip many well-intentioned Suttonians was frustration. It was immediately recognised that to meet the main task of increased housing, the 1945 total of 350,000 U.K. building industry manpower would have to be increased to 1½ million. The Government would open eleven training centres in six months' time and forty-four centres in the next 12 months. 200 Instructors were necessary straight away, eventually 2,000 were required.

An indication of more people about and perhaps a reason for raising the rates, was that refuse collected in the town in March/April 1945 was 307 tons more than the 1944 corresponding period.

MIXTURE OF REACTIONS TOWARDS AMERICAN SERVICEMEN

There was a mixture of sorrow and pleasure over the Upper Holland Road schools being returned in the first week of June by the American 'Military Authorities'. At least a Secondary School scheme could be completed. The additional accommodation enabled the compulsory school age to be raised to fifteen for the next academic year. Many American soldiers employed on postal duties were billeted in private houses, forming unforgettable friendships. A number of American Officers were introduced to members of Sutton Town Council by the Mayor, Councillor F. W. Terry. The Commanding Officer realised that the U.S. Forces personnel and Sutton Coldfield people "helped to bring the two great nations closer together". Yet, there were locals involved in stealing postal packets at the First Base Post Office and others stealing petrol from an American Army pool pump in Coleshill Road, used primarily for running coaches.

SUTTON'S FIRST POST WAR STRIKE

Less than two months after the War was over a Midland 'Red' event happened that has become forgotten in the mists of time. The introduction of new time schedules, which included late night services and Sunday morning buses, caused a strike at Dudley Garage. Sutton employees of the 1934 built garage came out in sympathy and spoke against the new working day of 13-15 hours. Many travellers to Sutton Park, finding there were no buses, complained to the B.M.M.O. Some small children had to walk more than two miles to reach school. A rather novel sight was heard and seen on Sunday 15th July, when a Midland 'Red' strike spokesman toured some Sutton streets with a car fitted with roof sited loudspeaker, expressing his colleagues' willingness "to go back to work as soon as the company was prepared to negotiate".

Many of the strikers did part-time work to make ends meet. Apparently work available was painting lamp posts and coal heaving by men. Women were offered potato picking and domestic work. Those who could afford a cinema visit saw "Going My Way" with Bing Crosby at the Odeon, "Tarzan's Secret Treasure" starring Johnny Weismuller, Maureen O'Sullivan and Barry Fitzgerald at the Empress and Anton Walbrook featured in "The Man From Morocco" at the Pavilion.

Six of the seven weddings recorded in the News of 23rd June included at least one service person.

THE FIRST POST WAR NATIONAL ELECTION

The War and foreign affairs were the dominating issues when Sir. John Mellor won the July 1945 seat for the Conservatives with 28,225 votes. F. W. Mulley, Labour, won 18,261 and Mrs Joyce Purser gained 2,043 for the Commonwealth Party. The majority was 9,964.

My brother and I benefited from the Charity grants in Sutton which were administered by Sutton Coldfield municipal charities. Up to £330 was spent annually on clothing for school children of deserving and needy persons resident in the Borough. I cannot remember receiving any clothing but I do recollect going with my mother to obtain footwear with a credit note used at Freeman Hardy and Willis.

Sutton was a two class town in the wake of World War II. As a council estate lad of 10 years old, I seemed to be content with my lot, though I realised years later my parents sacrificed so much for my brother and I. In August a house in Holifast Road was on the market for £2,500, with £10,000 properties available on the Four Oaks Estate.

In August the Canwell Horse show was revived, demonstrating the desire in the town to get back to normal, with promises that 1946 would present features and activities comparable to the pre-war extensive and very attractive Canwell Show programme. The likelihood of that seemed even more probable in mid-August.

YET MORE CELEBRATIONS

Against the emerging readjustments to family life, with breadwinners and sons and daughters back home, or expected shortly, there appeared a growing shortage of necessary accommodation. The Victory in Japan Day brought a respite with thanksgiving on Wednesday 15th August and day long celebrations. Sounds of music wafted across Central Sutton as Shirley Silver Band played in Vesey Memorial Gardens during the afternoon and evening. As families, we were amazed at the number of coloured electric lights. There were thousands, illuminating the Council House, Town Hall, Fire Station tower, Parade Shopping Centre and Parish Church. Dancing went on until a late hour in King Edward Square, enjoyed by a largely relieved crowd. Peace had finally come - it was really here, culminating in the end of the day's festivities with bonfires and fireworks heard well after midnight. For later generations, it would be difficult to comprehend the wide-eyed fascination of seeing so much peaceful light and noise. Even so, many felt fear as the fireworks exploded and momentary shafts of light rocketed heavenwards.

With the war over, the National Fire Service saw the opportunity to utilise some surplus equipment from Warwickshire County Council. However, there was a strong local protest against the use of the war sirens for any other purpose, even calling firemen to their posts in the event of any emergency.

TWO EMERGING ISSUES

Two emerging issues in the autumn and winter of 1945 were council housing and employment. The Council stressed the housing points system was a) based on need;

b) fair; c) equitable and d) free from suspicion of favouritism. After much discussion, the Health and Housing Committee had decided "the allocation of points was the only workable system". The major point earners in September 1945 were:- a married couple without a home of their own - 10 pts; their first child - 3 pts; further children - 4 pts each; expectant mother - counted as one child - 4 pts; overcrowding - does not allow couple their own bedroom - 3 pts; residence or employment in borough over 10 years - 3 pts; Service with H.M. Forces and being a War Widow allocated 2 pts each.

MATERNITY HOME NEEDED

The assumption that there would be a significant increase in Sutton Borough births was reinforced by the actions of the Mayoress, Marion Terry, and Mayor F. W. Terry, in advertising for donations to convert a building they knew was available into a maternity home. The need was urgent with housing conditions so difficult for all classes in the community, but particularly the wives of servicemen of all ranks. The first donation was £1,000 towards the £10,000 cost of alterations and equipment. Alan Smith wrote that "many Boldmere children in the war and in early post-war days were born in the Highfield Private Nursing Home". He was born in 1941 with brothers in 1944 and 1949.

Urgent calls for staff were made by Southerton and Son, Martineau and Smith of Coleshill Road, requiring boys, girls 14 - 18 years, men, women, full or part-time. The railways had vacancies in the West Midlands for Traffic porters, Goods porters, Horse carters, Callers up, Junior engine cleaners etc.

According to a Sutton Coldfield News leading article, employees who liked their job "were in the minority, being fortunate ones on earth". Apparently employers were losing their patience with staff going slow, resenting paying tax and finding ways of getting enough money to live on without giving a fair return in labour. In contrast, during February 1945, a commendable local transport scheme run by volunteers from the Boldmere Road Ambulance Depot, whose members met their own expenses, ran a service for Service personnel returning home, for example from Germany, Italy or India and arriving late at night in Birmingham.

Rather than leaving the Servicemen and women including an increasing number of Prisoners of War, to wait for public transport the next morning from New Street Station, a Birmingham branch of the Volunteer Transport Service conveyed them to Boldmere, where the Sutton volunteers took them in their own cars to Sutton locations and further away to Lichfield, Tamworth, Brownhills, Aldridge and Burton-on-Trent. 2 or 3 cars were available each night. In the first nine months, 1,750 were carried in this way, covering 20,000 miles. It was noted "that although the War was over - the work goes on".

W. Bromwich , Baker and Confectioner, Sutton Coldfield - Championship Winner - Dray, Driver and Horse. King Edward Square - 1930's? (T. Burton)

SUTTON'S AWARD WINNING BAKERY

The great, great grandson of William Bromwich, of the 1837 founded Bakery company, W. Bromwich & Son Ltd, was born in 1925, living at a Parade shop, near Moores. Donald, with his parents, moved to the late seventeenth century house on High Street, the front being converted into a shop with a cafe at the rear. The 1927 bakery was built by S. Pugh of Four Oaks. Don's father, Harold, developed the business. In 1941-43, Don delivered bread by horsevan to Lindridge Road, Whitehouse Common, Hartopp Road and Jockey Road, amongst others. Later, motor rounds went to Duntan Hall, with Wishaw in the South and as far as Blackbrook, near Weeford, in the North. The horses were called van horses of about fourteen and a half hands, being of mature age, used to motorised and noisy traffic conditions. "During the War" Donald informed me, "the horses were not stabled at night because of the risk of incendiary bombs as there were hay lofts above the stables". The Bakery rented two fields at the back of the old Sutton Coldfield Town Station "which was reached by the cinder path, beside the railway line from the Lichfield Road". Don remembered bread during the War was a mixture of white and brown, and called Farmhouse. Typical prices were 4d. for a 2 lb loaf and 2½d for a

1 lb loaf. Hovis cost 3d!. Don and his colleagues kept "cakes and buns under the seat in a special compartment". As cakes were in short supply, they were kept "for favoured customers, which" not surprisingly, "caused a bit of acrimony". It certainly did on our estate when word got out that Mrs So-and-So had cakes for the children's tea! Bromwich's sold the available big cakes for a shilling and buns for a similar amount, with twelve in a bag, one being a cream bun.

RESPONSIVE HORSES

The vans were painted and varnished occasionally. Another local firm, W. M. Chapman of Lichfield Road fitted solid rubber tyres or, when worn out, replaced by iron covered tyres. Don said "my uncle, who traded as W. H. Bromwich at Mere Green, had only 2 wheel vans." Another response Harold required of his horses was "they could be trusted to stand still until called, when they would walk up the street until told to stop. Which saved the man walking back." Two, however, did misbehave. "A colt when unattended, ended up out of town," and another "got tired of waiting near the end of the day and trotted with the van all the way home from Maney, along the Parade to the High Street depot".

On the rear of the horse drawn vans it proudly stated W. Bromwich had won awards for its products. Don's father, "was not disappointed at his son's decision not to continue the family business." Don advised me, "town life was not for me. I had always wanted to be a farmer." So Harold Bromwich sold the business "to Mr Wilfred Jones, who was an experienced caterer." Mr Jones retained the W. Bromwich name, and so continued the 1837 tradition.

Wilfred Jone's five year old son, David, found the Bakery and Stables "was a wonderful play area". There was a two floor brick building with flour room - stores and changing rooms on the upper level. The enticing aromas came from a large drawplate oven for the bread and also four ovens for other baking. Equipment included "three large dough troughs, large tables and other smaller machines." At the rear of the Bakery was a "long shed type building, used like a museum, with loads of riding equipment, accessories and brasses." Cobbled steps and a path led to the lower stables, where two large brown and white Clydesdale horses, Dolly and Tupp, and their two bakery carts were looked after.

David thought "in earlier years of W. Bromwich, five horses were used". In addition to the two Clydesdales "his father purchased a large grey hunter as a standby". His father rode the grey Hunter past the Town Hall one Sunday into the Park. The horse was high-spirited and instead of jumping the creek on the Meadow Platt, stopped dead, throwing his owner into the creek!

W. Bromwich & Sons Ltd, Dray in original livery, displayed at Worcestershire County Museum, Hartlebury, 2001. (Author)

SUTTON BAKERY ROUNDS

Some of the roundsmen over the years were "George Stewart (later to become Head Office Clerk), Harold Stanley, Ernie Allsopp, George Read and Jimmy Hope. Also George Jones. My brother-in-law's father was a doughman and also caretaker at the Old College, opposite the Fire Station". Typical rounds that came to David's mind were "Canwell and Wishaw, Walmley and the Reddicap, Clifton and Tudor Road, Tamworth Road and Little Sutton Lane, Wyvern Road and Anchorage Road". Bread he recalled "was around 4½d a loaf. The night staff at the Bakery were: Harold Perry, George Arthurs, Tommy Phipps, Albert Smith, Dick Thursfield and George Jones, who with his wife Gertrude, lived at the top of Trinity Hill, opposite the Church", where David sometimes used to call in after school.

Ced Lewis, a craftsman in wood and a volunteer restorer at the Worcestershire County Museum, Hartlebury, thought the W. H. Bromwich and Son Bakery van, exhibited at the Museum, was probably made in the early 1900's. The van remains in its 1946 condition when taken out of service. Wilfred Jones, prior to the Sutton Coldfield move, developed his speciality fruit cakes employed with Elizabeth the Chef in Leicester and Water Orton, as well as at Andrew Squires in Leicester.

An inside view looking towards the front of the Hartlebury exhibit. (Author)

For some years after the War, rationing remained the norm. David saw "normal working class people queueing down the High Street towards the Tuns waiting to use their Ration Books". Mr Jones "opened a cafe at the High Street shop so people could come in for tea and cakes". Young David also "remembered one occasion when Tommy Lawton, the England International footballer brought his Notts County F.C. round to tea - father took him round to the house and introduced him to me. What a thrill to shake hands with a great player".

FAVOURITE WELSH TEACHER

On arrival in Sutton, David attended the Primary School at the bottom of Mill Street which "was great". "My favourite teacher was Welsh, - her name was Miss Reece. She was very kind and I soon made some friends and was very happy there". Incidentally, the News reported that 1945 was the year Sutton Coldfield lost educational control of schools, going back to the founding of BVGS in 1541.

1945 was the year Tom Hunt was demobbed returning to his pre-war chimney sweeping business from Holland Street. Out came the screwing in rods, with brushes and sheets that had come through the War. Lilian said Tom "covered most streets in Sutton Coldfield. In those early post-war years he charged l/-d, for cottage chimneys, but 1/6d' for three storey houses like those in Somerville Road, Hartopp Road, Bakers Lane, Wyvern Road and Anchorage Road". Signalwoman Joan Price told me "Son Hunt", as he was known, "did a good job and cleared up after him". Lilian washed his sooty clothes and cloths which made her hands bleed in the icy weather. In the "quieter summer season, he did casual gardening to make ends meet", she added. The family made use of the Coleshill Street dispensary, making regular subscriptions. It was of help on many occasions.

Demob beckons for Tom Hunt (left) and mate, like thousands of other Warwickshire servicemen and women. (Mrs Lilian Hunt)

Mrs Margaret Beeson walked with other school children to the Civic Restaurant, eating the 5d. lunch in the Methodist Sunday School rooms. Margaret described the food "as good". Their family Doctor held surgery in his Birmingham Road home "with a small room attached used as a dispensary. It was a good thing if you were feeling a bit rough or had a child in tow". One of her "Jerome Road neighbours", she continued, "had her prescriptions from the Dispensary at the corner of Coleshill Street, opposite the Rectory. I often had to go there for her. There were long queues." There was a huge table in the centre of the rooms. On it would be pieces of knitting. Usually khaki scarves were in the process of being knitted. With a lot of people having a go, Margaret found "there would be a lot of mistakes and various widths due to uneven tensions, not to mention plenty of holes where people had dropped stitches. Helping to pass the time, I spent many Saturday mornings there!"

SALLY'S TURN

Frank Meigham's son informed me his father "was a delivery man for W. Bromwich & Sons for a short while after returning from war service in North Africa and Italy". The two Monday - Saturday rounds covered Mere Green and Four Oaks. Like other roundsmen, "the day's work included harnessing up the horse and feeding and stabling it at the end of the day." There were late finishes on Friday and Saturday when the cash from customers was collected. In Mr Meigham senior's notes he mentioned, "that the horse was named Sally and that she knew the two rounds - better than he did."

Sally made Frank aware on his first day, who was boss. At the end of the round, the notes recorded, "he turned the horse and van round ready to return and make the final delivery. Sally knew that turning round was the end of the journey and set-off homewards." The incident "caused much local merriment but he caught up with horse and cart." Thereafter he left "the horse facing the outward way until he had delivered the last loaf. "When the opportunity arose with Golby to have a delivery round with a Jowett van, he left. But Frank Meigham often recalled Sally's knowledge of the way home."

SUTTON PARK "FLASHER"

Olive remembered some cold winters at Princess Alice Orphanage at the end of the war. "Before going to school in the morning, during the winter months we did exercises in the yard", apparently making them feel warm in the classrooms.

Another way of encouraging good circulation was a generally enjoyable Saturday walk through Sutton Park with P.A.O. staff. However, extreme care was taken by the staff that the children were not confronted by a notorious male "flasher" that the rangers and police had not been able to apprehend.

Looking back at the P.A.O. life, Olive felt very privileged to be selected to present bouquets to special guests, alongside "a picked-out boy", making similar presentations, representing the children, staff and management.

S. Ashton Stray was employed in a senior role with the Sutton Coldfield Council, leaving after eleven years in 1945. He thought everything remained about the same in the first few months of 1945 "when nothing happened except for rejoicings at the approaching end of hostilities in Europe". Some locals still recall his significant local involvement in Sutton's life.

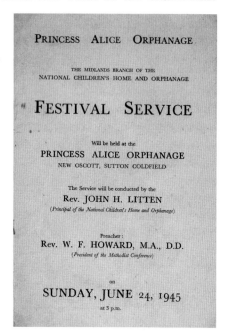

PRINCESS ALICE ORPHANAGE

THE MIDLANDS BRANCH OF THE
NATIONAL CHILDREN'S HOME AND ORPHANAGE

FESTIVAL SERVICE

Will be held at the
PRINCESS ALICE ORPHANAGE
NEW OSCOTT, SUTTON COLDFIELD

The Service will be conducted by the
Rev. JOHN H. LITTEN
(*Principal of the National Children's Home and Orphanage*)

Preacher:
Rev. W. F. HOWARD, M.A., D.D.
(*President of the Methodist Conference*)

on
SUNDAY, JUNE 24, 1945
at 3 p.m.

Front cover of the Princess Alice Orphanage Festival Service in 1945. (Janet Nixon)

Looking through 1945, B.B.C. Radio W.M. Network Gold Presenter John Platt named three songs as the most popular in the year the Second World War ended. They were 'Cruising down the River', 'April Showers', and 'We'll gather lilacs in the Spring'.

NO 216 M.U.'S SUCCESSFUL C.O. AND TEAM

On Tuesday 11th December 1945, Sutton's R.A.F. base had an important inspection by Air Marshal Sir Arthur Barratt, K.C.B., C.M.G., M.C., One of our contributors, Mr Sargent, cherishes two letters written in January 1946, advising the Officer in Command at Whitehouse Common, Wing Commander T. J. Kinna, of the Air Marshal's report. Referring to this report, the C.O. was advised "I am sending you this note to let you know that he was very satisfied indeed with everything he saw". The report continued "During the War, whilst at the Air Ministry, I saw all the I.G.'s reports, and found them most extraordinarily interesting . However, I don't recollect seeing one about any unit which reflected a really well run and administered unit as does the report on No. 216 M.U.

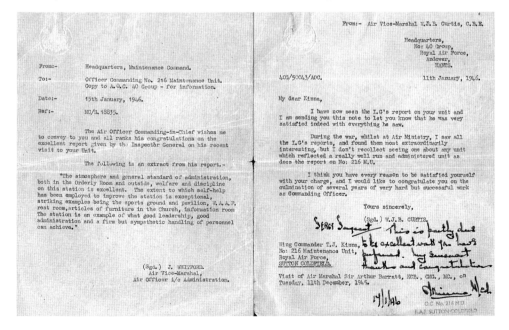

R.A.F. 216 M.U. - Reports of an excellently run unit, with comments by the C.O. to Sgt. Sargent for his efforts. (W. D. Sargent)

"I think you have every reason to be satisfied yourself with your Command, and I would like to congratulate you on the culmination of several years of very hard and extremely successful work as Commanding Officer". The written addition to the letter by his C.O. still means a lot to William Sargent. "Sergeant Sargent. This is partly due to the excellent work you have performed. My sincerest thanks and congratulations", signed and dated 17.1.46. This is an extract from R.A.F. H.Q., Maintenance Command - "The atmosphere and general standard of administration, both in the Orderly Room and outside, welfare and discipline on this station is excellent. The extent to which self-help has been employed to improve the Station is exceptional. Several striking examples being the sports ground and pavilion, W.A.A.F. rest room, articles of furniture in the Church, information room. The station is an example of what good leadership, sound administration and a firm but sympathetic handling of personnel can achieve".

Chapter Three

1946 – 87,000 Types of R.A.F. Equipment

Mr Sargent was demobbed in February 1946, with the knowledge that his efforts with No 216 M.U. had been highly successful and praised by the R.A.F. hierarchy and his own Commanding Officer. He also seemed to be content with No 5 B.C. Birmingham North!

William, a former G.W.R. employee at Swindon, remained in the town, with his Suttonian wife and their child. I wondered if the family attended No 216 M.U. Open Day later that year, when the public for the first time learned of all the services offered by the Whitehouse Common base. Since July 1942, despatches of equipment had been sent by rail, road, sea and air, including parachutes and airborne lifeboats. Visitors were advised of large numbers of parachutes dropped in most parts of the world during the war. 87,000 different types of equipment were held at 216 M.U., the Sutton Coldfield News reported. The Station's W.A.A.F. Band, always in great demand, played to enthusiastic service audiences, "in many parts of the country". 216 M.U. had its own small farm, and growing its own vegetables, sold £1,245 worth of produce in 1945.

Mr H. S. Higgins with another R.A.F. Unit was demobbed in 1946, having served as a cook. Before the War his profession was that of a photographer, having trained with Speights on the Parade. Back in civilian life once more, he took many wedding pictures and portraits in Boldmere, specialising in passport photos.

Pamela, with her parents since 1937 at The Fox Inn, Walmley, found the car park was adequate for 20 - 30 cars in the early post war years because "there was not much

James H. Bacon - Licensee of the Fox Inn, Walmley, 1937-1954. c. 1940. (Mrs P.D. Done)

car ownership" at the time. The pub had "excellent living facilities, with double outer timber doors and swing glass doors leading into the public bar etc". Although her parents had "very little leisure time", her father was a member of the local Bowls, Snooker and Golf club, plus enjoying playing football for Sutton Town". Pamela thought that as The Fox provided food for its patrons, the family "probably had a little more food" than others. The pub had a 'dumb waiter' lift that went from the scullery and living room down to the lounge and cellar, which ran the full lengths of the property.

CANWELL BABY HOSPITAL'S NEW DRUG

Mrs Dove remembered "the local G.P. was Dr. Ramsdale who held surgery at his house on the corner of Walmley Ash/Eachelhurst Road. Opposite was the old Vicarage where Rev A. Weeks resided. Further along Walmley Ash" she continued, "was a private school called The Shrubbery".

Mr & Mrs Steventon were further members of "The Rectory Road Dispensary. It was a very useful asset, for a few pence a week with their dentist being Mr Evans on the corner of Maney Hill Road". Their three children attended Duke Street, Victoria Road and the Riland Bedford Schools, with them all having "the school meals and free milk".

In 1946, Canwell Hall Baby Hospital expanded its age range from babies to fourteen year olds. (Susie King Collection)

Susie King at Canwell Hall Children's Hospital, said "that shortly after the close of the War, a new extremely effective treatment became available to their young patients". Susie went on "a treatment successfully administered to forces personnel in the Second World War was penicillin. It was particularly beneficial to the babies with pneumonia". She considered the new drug to be a "precious" help for children. Oxygen tents were a valuable initiative, the big ones over six months old and more, whereas the Queen Charlotte Hospital type was placed over the cribs of tiny children. It was in 1946, the Night Superintendent informed me that "at the request of hospital authorities, Canwell expanded their age range from five up to fourteen year olds".

PLAYING FIELD CIRCUS SITE

According to Margaret Beeson, née Wilkins "when the Circus came to Sutton immediately after the War, it was always sited on the Holland Road playing fields. The children would go over there to help the circus staff in the hope of getting a free ticket! Sir. Robert Fossett's Gigantic Circus and Zoo were at the Play field site in the spring. Adults admission was 1/6d - 7/6d; children 1s - 3/6d. I remember helping at least one circus there and gaining entrance to the circus and zoo, but the way the 'professional' staff cared for the animals was at times appalling. No doubt it was a hard life, with short turn round targets and perhaps some difficult animals, yet the treatment and attitudes, plus swearing, left a lot to be desired. Margaret found "we had to queue for what seemed like hours to get in but there were the playing field swings and slides and see-saw to play on whilst waiting".

John Dennis was at BVGS between 1944 - 50, getting chased by farmers and gamekeepers around the New Hall Estate area during the holidays. He bought his first suit at Burton's Parade shop for £10, and an overcoat at £15 from Hepworths. John remembers having a mole

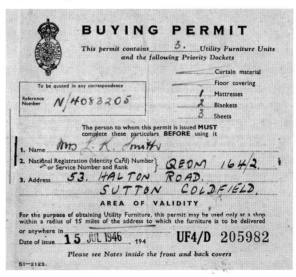

Buying permit for a mattress, blankets and sheets. (Alan Smith)

removed at the Sutton Cottage Hospital, where Alan Smith had his tonsils sorted out. Alan said "I can still remember the gargle. It was some foul tasting red liquid. I was in a large room with other children". He added "the one consolation was jelly for tea!" Margaret, thinking of treats, recalled that when "Woolworths had a delivery of ice cream, the queue would be right around the shop". The items being sold were "usually the small polar bear ice creams which fitted into a cornet. At times we had queued only to find they had sold out before my turn". "Trows", she remembered "made their own ice cream".

I certainly queued for Trows ice cream, served in a glass dish and slowly devoured with appropriate spoon in the milk bar looking towards the railway line.

THE ADVANTAGES OF PREFABS.

At the beginning of 1946, the Mayor, Councillor Mayall, opened the first of four temporary homes on a Four Oaks Common Road site, handing the keys to Mr & Mrs Neville Lampert. One hundred would be erected at seven points, under the Housing Temporary Accommodation Act, 1944. In answer to that type of housing "being much maligned, persons should inspect them first". The Mayor laid down a challenge to the sceptics, that they would find "kitchen fittings which would be the envy of 75% of Sutton Coldfield housewives". Sutton also witnessed the temporary extension of amenities in the Park at the start of the year, though only for six days! Skating was enjoyed over those days on the pools, most popular being Wyndley, Blackroot, Bracebridge. Once the word was out, Ice Hockey teams from Birmingham held their league matches on the town pools. Skating did not finish with the darkness, because enthusiastic skaters weakened their batteries playing the car lights on to the ice. Sutton Coldfield youngsters, as inventive as usual, shaped tree branches into sticks, playing their own version of ice hockey. Sutton Coldfield Town Council had a mammoth reconstruction programme of their own in changing eight committees at the cost of £378,000.

A SMOULDERING PRE-WAR GRIEVANCE

A national railway advertisement by the G.W.R., L.M.S. L.N.E.R. and S.R. advised railway passengers - we became customers 50 years later - that if trains were late or overcrowded, or both, it was probably due to a shortage of trained staff, carriages, locomotives or inferior quality coal. Passengers were asked to remain patient as it "will take time to restore pre-war standards". For a while Sutton Council, not satisfied with the public transport provision in the borough, explored the possibility of operating their own bus services. Apparently, negotiations with the Midland 'Red', clarified that the council "did not have the necessary powers to effect this". However, the large Omnibus company, encouraged by employees returning from the Forces, and new vehicles promised for the summer, intended to improve the 107 service and introduce double decker buses on some other routes. A smouldering grievance from pre-war years was fanned into flame with the public demand for an omnibus centre in the town. Early in 1939 it was "deferred until the proposals relative to the Parade by-pass would be completed". Councillor A.G.B. Owen thought it was "deplorable" that the council kept deferring the question. He argued that they "should decide the location for a future omnibus centre". Tempers of some Suttonians and bus operators remain inflamed over a similar issue in the New Millennium!

POST OFFICE INNOVATION - '999'

The News recorded in an early March edition that the Post Office had introduced an emergency telephone number of '999' to contact the services of Fire, Police, Ambulance or Mines Rescue in the Birmingham telephone area. Locally, the Police were forced to exhort car owners to move their vehicles because they impeded traffic along the Parade and Mill Street "causing vehicles to frequently run on footways".

Bracebridge Pool was a delightful place as some Post-War restrictions eased.
(Birmingham Library Services / P. Bryant)

SEARCH FOR STARS

Much interest was shown in the Carol Levis Show 'Search for Stars' held in Sutton Coldfield Town Hall. From the nineteen acts, judges chose nineteen year old Miss Yvonne Allen and Mr Alan F. Thompson to go forward to the regional final. Mr Levis' brother, Cyril, was on hand to congratulate the two winners. Mr & Mrs Woodcock wondered if they were owners of one of the first caravans in the town, a Permanatou, a four berth which they took to Tal-y-bont for a number of years with their daughters. Sutton Council accepted with regret the resignation of the Town's Medical Officer of Health, Dr. J. H. Wright, after having served the Borough for twenty seven years. He resigned because of permanent ill health.

SUNDAY CINEMA VOTE

Warwickshire C.C. had granted the local cinemas a licence to 31st May 1946, to open from 4 - 10.00pm on Sundays to screen films because "of circumstances arising out of the War". Out of the 33,746 qualified to vote, only 4,179 bothered on polling day, to decide whether Sunday Cinema opening should continue. 3,243 voted yes, with 936 against. The News described it as 'Cinema Poll Apathy'. The majority of 29,567 were apparently disinterested. Alderman A. E. Terry was active in encouraging more feminine influence on the Sutton Council, particularly with committees dealing "with women's questions". Four months later, Mrs K. M. Garrard "was a proud woman", becoming the Mayor. Sutton M.P., Sir John Mellor, told the 'House' he had found from "very exhaustive inquiries in his constituency that not one single person wanted a Victory J. Day", as he criticised the Government's celebration plans.

SUTTON'S AWAKENING SPORTS SCENE

1946 saw the revival of a number of sports. Although Sutton Coldfield Cricket Club, under very great difficulty, kept going during the war, at the A.G.M. in its ninety ninth year, many old members from the Forces were welcomed, with normal playing activities to resume in 1947. The club had a twenty one year lease from Sutton Council for the Rectory Park ground, with arrangements in hand to appoint a full time groundsman. Full public access to Rectory Park was available in the summer. After severe damage to the Pavilion, it had been made more secure. The Tudor Bowling Club's 1946 season opened with a large number of members participating. Interest in Boldmere St. Michael's F.C. 1946/7 season was causing excitement in the town with the club accepting an invitation to rejoin the prestigious

Weeford Picnic - Typical of early Post War picnic - Jones family, who bought out the High Street Sutton, Bromwich the Bakers in 1945. (David Jones)

Central Amateur League in which it had successfully competed for two years prior to the War. The 1946 membership of the Old Veseyan Association was claimed to be higher than 1939 "and definitely stronger financially." A friendly match between Sutton Coldfield C.C. and a Warwickshire County XI was extremely well attended, the visitors making "a sporting declaration". With the gradual availability of more men as leaders, a Scouts exhibition in Sutton Town Hall promoted what scouting organisations offered to local boys and young men, including some excellent recreational pursuits.

TO BUILD OR NOT TO BUILD?

Concern had been expressed in the town because of the number of early post-war licences granted for building, resulting in the majority not fulfiling the requirements. The Ministry of Health reiterated their instructions that developers must make early effective starts. The failure to do that, meant 143 local licences were cancelled including 128 new houses. Fortunately the temporary housing programme was nearly complete in September, when ninety two of the hundred were handed over. Another building innovation was the construction of fifty two

British Iron and Steel Federation houses in the town. Thirty three squatters in the Walmley Ash huts and ninety six persons squatting at the Streetly Gun site, had some housing points forfeited because council officials considered the two groups had satisfactory "water and sewerage arrangements".

The Midland 'Red' urgently advised the local population that in an effort to improve the Sutton area bus services, accommodation was needed for recruited drivers and conductors at the Upper Holland Road garage.

The Town's refuse plant, over thirty year old, was to be replaced by a new facility. Sanction was given to raise a loan of £17,750.

HIGHBURY THEATRE'S CONFERENCE

Louise MacNeice spoke on behalf of many amateur theatre managements and patrons that television was likely to have an adverse effect on local non-commercial productions. At the third Highbury Theatre Conference, the Poet, and Radio dramatist "was concerned with the possibility of T.V. taking the power of the spoken word and sound from Radio by the stressing of vision". Such a result, Louise warned was "regrettable". Before the end of the decade, her visionary statement would be even more pertinent, radiating from Sutton Coldfield throughout the Midlands. In the professional arena, Birmingham Hippodrome hosted Robb Wilton, whereas the cinemas offered: Danny Kaye in 'Wonderman' at the Odeon, the Empress showing

Wyndley café, a safe place for children and adults to be refreshed. (Arthur

'Lady on the Train' featuring Deanna Durbin, Edward Everett Horton and David Bruce and the Pavilion screened Van Johnson, Esther Williams in 'The Thrill of a Romance!' A few weeks later, the Empress was proud to show 'Brief Encounter', starring Celia Johnson, Trevor Howard and Stanley Holloway.

In August 1946, children who went in to the Sutton Park paddling pool were at risk of serious injury. Twenty one children suffered cut feet from broken glass and jagged open ended cans. Eight of the injuries required outpatient treatment at Sutton Hospital. Park Foresters cleared the "stream which runs for almost a mile". A few days later along a sixty yard stretch, they "produced two more barrow loads of glass".

PERTURBED YOUTH LEADERS

There was "great consternation among Sutton Youth Leaders over the lack of adequate sports grounds for youth activities". Five groups wished to enter a league competition but the non availability of their own or use of a ground prevented their acceptance by the league selection committee. The youth groups could have been jealous of Sutton Town F.C., formed in January 1879, and suspended at the close of the 1939/40 season, being offered the Coles Lane ground for the first two years rent free. In addition, the Sutton Council agreed to provide a "stand in a state of good repair".

1946 Boldmere Infant School Reception Class. Class teacher Miss Davies (left) and Head teacher, Miss Keeling (right), Barry Chapman is in centre backrow. Contributor Alan Smith is second from right at the front. Martin Jones had a mat to himself. (Alan Smith)

POSSIBLE SUTTON BOUNDARY CHANGES

Sutton Coldfield Council were in contentious debate concerning larger areas of land, bearing in mind local authority boundary changes. They were opposed to Aldridge wanting to take over part of Sutton's area. Yet at the same time, Meridian (M.D.C.) were angry to learn, Sutton had a desire to include the M.D.C. area within the Sutton boundary.

With the population increasing in the West Midlands, the popularity of Sutton park visits grew to 554, 444 in a twelve months period in 1945-1946. Data recorded 298 head of cattle grazed in the park costing their owners £32 1s. 9d. Cattle and horses had to be removed by 31st October each year.

A new departure in the Warwickshire Library Service was to have its first record section opened in the Sutton Central library with an initial stock of one thousand records. W. H. Bromwich gained two 1sts and one 2nd prize in the British Isles Confectionery awards at Bolton. A junior member of staff received a silver medal, an encouraging sign for the future.

The year 1947 was to see the emergence of a massive housing development, a model that attracted many visitors from the United Kingdom and abroad. 1946 closed with rationing still much in evidence. Though with limited resources, Suttonians enjoyed peace over Christmas, reflecting on a long, hard won war.

Chapter Four

1947 – INNOVATIVE METHODS AROUND RATIONING

The severe winter of 1946-47 began in November 1946, carrying on into March 1947, causing problems for everybody, people going to work, shopping, children getting to school, journeys by cycle, motor cycle and car involved travelling on hazardous roads. Local public transport services were at times disrupted. Trades people found it difficult in the early part of 1947 to make reliable deliveries of bread, milk and coal. Mrs Hunt was impressed with the initiative of the Co-op milkman where, because of the terrible road conditions up Farthing Lane, he left the horse and van at a safe spot. With a young helper he manhandled a sledge up the incline full of customers' milk.

The severity of the winter gave temporary snow clearing work to many in the town. The Borough Surveyor reported between January 30th - February 8th some men worked up to seventy hours during a week. All casual labourers, and all applicants from the Labour Exchange were given work immediately - forty two in all, up to 12th February.

Mrs L. Hunt was impressed with the Co-op milkman making his deliveries by sledge in Farthing Lane during atrocious weather. (Birmingham Library Services)

PIPER! PIPER!

Mrs Hunt noted that Len Robinson from his Mere Green newsagents shop delivered Sunday papers along Lichfield Road into the town. Len's disabled son assisted him. Dr. Raines spoke of Mr Robinson - "he used to sell newspapers on a Sunday morning from a low, two-wheeled cart drawn by a pony. His arrival in Riland Road from Rectory Road direction was accompanied by the cry of 'Piper! Piper!' and he always drew up outside No. 65, about half-past ten." John recalled that he was "a heavily-built man with a fresh complexion, in his sixties and wearing a cap". Len apparently carried on with the Sunday deliveries until at least 1950.

Another contributor, Jenny Steiger, "remembered" a greengrocer frequently visiting St. Michael's Road in Boldmere in the mid-forties". Phil Budd walked at the side of the horse, that pulled "an open cart filled with vegetables of all kinds". Jenny described Mr Budd, "of swarthy, handsome appearance with dark curly hair which hung over his forehead". He called out his wares as he walked down the street. Each autumn, rather than see his juicy plums go soft and inedible on the cart, he threw handfuls to children like Jenny. She commented "most folk didn't have the money for such luxuries as plums during those lean after-war years".

'AGIONI!'

A further type of tradesman that we had down Jerome Road, came back to mind from Jenny Steiger's account of "the rag and bone man to whom we all referred as 'Agioni' because that's what his call for 'Any old rags' sounded like to us". That man was "short, dumpy, red-faced, wearing a flat cap that looked as though it had come from his cart". She added, "and probably had!" Like many hundreds of kids in Sutton, the St. Michael's Road children received "day old chicks in return for a good bundle of rags. Later on, a goldfish was the exchange". We used to keep the chicks warm in our Jerome Road back kitchen from the heat radiating from the oven and lounge coal fire.

Thinking of Jenny's chicks, "some of the chicks lasted well, we had three in total. One died fairly soon, but the cock was with us for a couple of years, before he ended up on the table at Christmas". The children never learnt it was one of the household pets until years later! Their hen laid eggs for several years.

COAL BOARD CHANGES

Coal, in 1947, remained a major source of heating homes and fuelling power stations. The West Midlands Divisional Coal Board assumed control of the one hundred and fifty plus collieries in our home county of Warwickshire, also North and South Staffordshire. During the year there was a serious shortage of power with domestic customers being requested to reduce their consumption of electricity at peak hours. The Midland 'Red' sent out an urgent call to factories and large businesses to advise them in plenty of time of the hours they were to work and when they needed work services. Some companies had given the public transport providers less than twenty four hours notice, which consequently disrupted the schedules, resulting in their inability to fulfil contracts.

SUTTON'S MODEL HOUSING ESTATE

Faced with a growing demand for council provided housing in the 1930's, Sutton Corporation agreed to the purchase of land for the Falcon Lodge Estate on 31st May 1937. Mr Frank Cattell, the owner of the Falcon Lodge Farm, accepted the £37,500 price, but the purchase was not completed until September 1946. However, the Estate drainage scheme by Tarmac Ltd at £4,716.4.3d, had been done in September 1938, which the Council paid for. In October 1939, the Air Ministry paid towards a larger sewer to include the drainage needs of the Balloon Barrage site. The owner of the Falcon Lodge Estate agreed to pay the rate of £4 per house when the development took place. Incidentally the Air Ministry also funded the resurfacing of a road because of the wear and tear by large vehicles and equipment when the Balloon Barrage site was being built.

A RANCOROUS DISPUTE

Local Sutton Historian, Mr Roger Lea, advised me that Mr Cattell in 1946, according to Sutton Council, owed £500 relating to the sewers. The District Valuer gained a tentative agreement from the landowner to pay £250. In a feature, 'A Look at Falcon Lodge' published in the Sutton Coldfield Local History Society Spring 1974 issue of proceedings, Mrs Marian Baxter noted a "Rancorous dispute between the owner and the Corporation over liability for the sewerage costs of the Falcon Lodge development". Mr Cattell was so incensed by the Council's (in his opinion) unjust demands, that he revoked his earlier decision to present his extensive collection of Sutton historical data and railway memorabilia to the town. At one stage he had the use of the 1879 Midland Railway, upside building (Birmingham direction) of Sutton Coldfield Town station, where he kept many railway items.

The Model of Falcon Lodge Estate at the Sutton Coldfield Civic Exhibition in 1947. (Birmingham Library Services)

Sutton Coldfield Town Council chose concrete rather than macadam roads on the Falcon Lodge Estate. (Birmingham Library Services)

CONCRETE RATHER THAN TARMACADAM

The 'News' reported in 1947 that the Falcon Lodge Estate development covered 198 acres, having an overall density of 8 houses to the acre, allowing room for 1,560 houses. The plan included 20 shops, grouped in a central position on the estate. Other amenities would be a Church, social centre, cinema, old people's hall and licenced premises. Acknowledging the obvious need for educational provision, school sites were identified on adjacent land sections. Further, subject to Ministry of Health approval, 2 bungalows for disabled servicemen were also to be included. The Town Planning Committee during the preparations for the estate decided to construct concrete roads in preference to tarmacadam. In the near future the Falcon Lodge Estate became a blueprint for other developments both here and abroad.

LEFT WITH A FRENCH POODLE

A fashion conscious young lady walked along the Parade with probably the first small black French poodle in Sutton after the War. Arriving at a shop, which beckoned her in, she handed the lead to her embarrassed boyfriend. Without the responsibility of the expensive pet animal, she indulged in time consuming, enjoyable shopping. She anticipated that the boyfriend would have the time to get to know the dog by the time she re-emerged. To her absolute surprise and disgust, the boyfriend was surrounded by attractive young women, enthralled by the lovely poodle and its charming owner. In the future, she thought twice about leaving the dog with him. She considered the animal would be safe, but she may lose him!

FOLLOWING THE SQUATTERS

Patricia Barratt was engaged to an Observer in the Fleet Air Arm who was serving abroad for much of the time. Following his demob in 1946, they began to make wedding plans.

"Following the War", Patricia wrote, "times were still very austere. There had been no building of new houses. During the War, most married couples were living with parents or in rented rooms. Patricia considered they were 'lucky' to purchase a semi-detached house. It was structurally sound but "in a very poor and dilapidated condition". Nevertheless, it was still priced at £900. The property had been occupied "by squatters who had wreaked havoc," the window frames were rotten, the bath had rusted through and "the general smell was appalling." With the windows replaced to protect them from the elements, they stripped off six layers of wallpaper "from the whole house, which boasted eights rooms as well as a long hall and landing". It was during the bitter winter of January - March 1947 they worked away. The smell came from the "flour and water paste which over the years had become sour. We came triumphantly to the last layer of paper - and with that out fell the plaster!" Mrs Price admitted "I think if we had not been in love and proud of our 'house' we would have walked out at that stage, but youth is resilient and we began work on replastering". With the assistance of the two families, including the complete re-wiring of the house, courtesy of Patricia's father's company, T. Barratt & Co, the property became two flats.

GAS TO ELECTRICITY

Thomas Barratt's business was well-known in Sutton Coldfield, with a radio shop in 1919 at No 32 High Street, though more readers will recall the company's elegant building at the top of the Parade on the corner of Mill Street and Station Street, previously the Gas offices. Incidentally "many of the large houses in Sutton and the surrounding areas were converted from gas to electricity by T. Barratt & Co", Mrs Price advised me. Later, Barratt's acquired premises at 11/13 Station Street, Sutton, converting them into an electrical workshop for the repair of radio and household appliances, and subsequently television. Over the years we used Barratt's services. Passengers waiting for Tamworth and Nottingham Midland 'Red' buses, often looked across at the Mill Street showroom from the 110 and X99 bus stops.

JUNGLE COMBAT - BACK TO SUTTON

George Robbins, a former fourteen year old railway porter at Sutton Coldfield moved to parcel deliveries from New Street station before war service took him to India via South Africa and then Burma. With vivid memories of jungle combat "where he lost many friends", not surprisingly it took the trainee signalman at Sutton Coldfield some time to adjust back to life in Sutton.

Leonora, usually known as 'Joyce', a private in the Auxiliary Territorial Service (A.T.S.) corresponded regularly with George from his posting to the far east. They still have hundreds of letters from those times - all checked by the military. Similar to other Post War married couples mentioned in this volume, rationing restrictions were encountered. There had been "much saving up and swapping of food coupons." Joyce thinks they "had a special sugar allowance for the wedding." After the Holy Trinity Church Service in March 1947, there was a reception at the groom's sisters' home in Boldmere. There followed a week's honeymoon in Blackpool. Joyce was well placed for shopping on return from Lancashire, living "in a one room flat over Wimbushes at 92, The Parade." The facilities were "a gas

Demobbed and Married - George and Joyce Robbins represent hundreds of local couples, including service personnel, married in 1945 - 1947.

ring and fire, use of shared bathroom on a lower floor." The Bride had inherited "my parents furniture so we had to buy very little. Rationing was very tight." Joyce related an advantage to their flat. "I was in a very good place to spot deliveries of any off ration goodies as our room overlooked what was then Smarts the Butchers." When Mrs Robbins saw the delivery van arrive, she smartly nipped down the Wimbushes stairs, being "first in the queue for sausages, offal, etc." Living above a Bakers, supplemented their meagre rations with dried bread, turned into toast, with a liberal covering of dripping.

SIGNALMAN'S SURPRISE

Joyce "quite quickly became pregnant in that one room!" Sutton's Housing Manager, Dick Hardy, went to the bed-sit to verify the couple's situation, Joyce wearing "her first maternity smock, which all expectant mothers wore in those days." Extra points were gained for a) "George being raised in Sutton Coldfield" and b) "us both being in the forces." When a subsequent letter arrived from the housing department, the wife felt her husband should know immediately. "I hopped straight on a bus", Joyce informed me "and ran down the Four Oaks station platform waving the letter," to George the duty signalman. As expected "George was equally thrilled, and later we went to collect the keys from the Town Hall," for a new two bedroomed semi-detached house in Blackberry Lane. They felt very fortunate. It had a nice location, near the 102 bus route - 2½d to Sutton, with front, side and rear gardens. To their surprise the weekly council rent at 16/- was only 3/6 more than the one room Parade bed-sit.

POST-WAR INNOVATIVE MEASURES

Mrs Shelagh Joynes as a young girl spent many Saturdays, on a milk round, assisting Doris, delivering bottles of sterilised milk along Station Road, The Boulevard, Green Lanes and Boldmere Road. A route around Boldmere which Millie, the fairly old horse knew well, was Highbridge Road, Weston Road, Eastern and Beacon Roads. When Doris and Shelagh took milk to a big house on the corner of the Boulevard, they were only allowed to go to the back door, "even to collect the money". At a more friendly call at another "big house, we were given fruit cake and a drink". There was a partial drawback "but we had to sit in the garden shed". On the quiet side roads, Doris handed over the reins. "There was no pay, just for interest". Wistfully, she recalled "quite a lot of my schoolfriends had their own ponies". Amongst sporting activities the girls took part in at Hollies Collegiate School, Canwell, was rugger! Shelagh praised "the very good school dinners from home grown food" at the mixed private school for up to eighteen year olds. Mrs Joynes and her mother, like thousands of other mothers and daughters in the town in times of post war rationing, found innovative ways of producing clothing. They made T shirts out of dusters. Shelagh's mother took down some curtains "to make a two-piece suit, and made underwear out of parachute silk."

A sample priority docket, not for Mrs Price's bedroom suite, but one utility mattress. (Alan Smith)

Mrs Price, in preparation for her autumn wedding, painted, assisted by husband-to-be, the walls with distemper (commonly known as "wallop"). Wallpaper was non-existent. The house was fresh and clean - and so began furnishing. With their prized 'dockets' they had a choice of a bedroom suite or a dining suite. They opted for a bedroom suite and a second hand dining suite.

Patricia said that "weddings at that time were much simpler than today, 2002". "My father donated his clothing coupons for my utility wedding dress which was figured satin and cost £9/-/-". That was Mrs Price's-to-be wages for two weeks. She "borrowed the veil and re-silvered my dancing shoes. The bridesmaids' dresses were hired."

THE CORNER SHOP

Mr John Crockett, the Manager of Hurrells, the Grocers, on Sutton Parade, left to take over one of the two corner shops near our Jerome Road home, with wife Sally, in 1947. I was 12 when the Crocketts became part of the local community, with son Michael. Catering for council house residents in Jerome Road, Ebrook Road, side avenues, and people from the Wylde Green end of Coles Lane, they gained an intimate knowledge of hundreds of families, becoming aware of whom they could trust and those they would only sell provisions to for cash. Like many estate shops, local events and gossip were swopped, but John and Sally knew when confidential news was to be kept to themselves. Continuing the rationing theme, Mrs Crockett told me "During rationing we had to check all stock at delivery, also take coupons for all goods rationed, these had to be sent or taken to the Food Office, when supplying emergency rations for soldiers on leave. These had to be applied for to replace goods for regular customers". The monitoring of the rationing scheme included regular visits by "Food Officers and Weights and Measures Inspectors".

Park Road Congregational Church in the 1940's. (Janice Moore)

Within a short while of managing the shop, they "introduced a full grocery and provisions service, in addition to taking on customers ration requirements". In the 1950's, The News was to print a number of articles of what happened to the small independent shops on the Parade and the estate community shops, with the development and popularity of the emerging supermarkets.

TOO MUCH LIGHT

In 1947, not only was rationing a way of life for shopkeepers, the restrictions on the use of electricity were severe at times. One lively, jovial shop owner, who helped shoppers with his good-humoured banter, through various times of crisis, was a local fruiterer. He had a business towards the Park Road end of the Parade. Unfortunately, George Rose fell foul of the influential Ministry of Fuel and Power. According to his defence in court, "his assistants needed more light to count the money," and Mr Rose "thought the regulations had been removed". The court heard that the premises at the time of two inspections had seventeen lights on. A Ministry regulation only permitted 675 watts to be used, whereas the fruit shop staff were using 3,400 watts. Counsel for the M.O.F.P. reminded the Court "practically the only way to make electricity in this country is from coal". There was a £2 fine on both charges for "unnecessary and wasteful use of fuel".

One of an excellent nostalgic collection of paintings by the late George Gilbert, purchased by Sutton Coldfield Library, photographed by Dr. John Raines. Mr Gilbert provides an accurate record of Pattisons, Trows and Manders. (Sutton Coldfield Library, George Gilbert, Dr. John Raines)

An example of the continuing spirit of 'dig for victory' came from the first post war A.G.M. of the 1886 established Sutton Coldfield and District Gardeners Mutual Improvement Association, where the membership had grown to 159. It enabled and encouraged local gardeners and allotment holders to grow and experiment with vegetables, fruit and flowers, and so a new centre of interest and activity had been born.

IMPROVED BUS SERVICES

Midland 'Red' news featured at regular intervals early in 1947. Some local services improved when staff and vehicles became available. The company decided to invest in three staff hostels for employees recruited outside the West Midlands at: Leamington, Bearwood and Sutton Coldfield. Permission was granted for a £30,000 large scale garage extension to the rear of the Upper Holland Road premises, though a timber licence was not approved. The 112 Birmingham-Sutton-Lichfield-Burton-on-Trent route became hourly in the day, taking one hour and forty minutes to complete.

FOOTBALL FEVER

With the restrictions of the War still fresh in most people's minds, the freedom to watch football matches without fear of air raids at local grounds encouraged folk to enjoy the spring and autumn evening

Sutton's adopted Glaswegian artist, George Gilbert sits patiently to be photographed by his Suttonian born wife. (Mrs. R. Gilbert)

nights, watching the increasing number of team games taking place. In the company of a few hundred others, I made my way to Rectory Road to support Sutton Athletic F.C. One game that caused much excitement was Athletic's win over near rivals Walmley, 3-1. Boldmere St. Michael's gained fame, reaching the F.A. Amateur Cup semi-final against Worthing in London. The 'Mikes' reached an early postwar milestone by fielding a 14-15 year olds junior team. At the A.G.M. of the Athletic, with much pride, it was noted in their first season, 1946-47, the Division One League Championship was won, without defeat. They also won the Britton Cup.

This freedom to investigate our local environment in relative safety was experienced by John Tidmarsh. From his bedroom windows he could see the beauty of Sutton Park beckoning, a mile away. From 1947, with his brother and their friends, "we explored every inch on foot or bicycle. In time, I liked to think if dropped into the park anywhere, blindfold and left, a couple of minutes after the blindfold had been removed, I would know my location."

PARKIE AVOIDANCE

The group "got to know all the 'Parkies'", being particularly alert to encounters with them, when cycling through the woods, "which was forbidden!" The chums used to "vie with each other to see how fast they could cycle right round the Park, using roads that ran just outside or inside the boundary fence". John never got round in less than thirty minutes. His particular favourite spot, probably like many other Suttonians and visitors, was the "old encampment up behind Blackroot Pool". Although I went into the park many times during the twenty-eight years I lived in the Royal Town, on the one occasion joining a midnight ramble, I soon lost any idea of my location. Perhaps the difference was that I never cycled in the Park, trying to avoid Park Keepers!

BRITISH RESTAURANT CLOSURE

In contrast to the opening up of activities and leisure opportunities, the British Restaurant operating in the Methodist Hall, in South Parade, closed. The reason given by the Town Council was "local caterers were now capable of providing sufficient meals". "It was suggested a dinner should cost 1/9d". 300 odd people ate regularly in the wartime introduced service. The Ministry of Food heralded the coming of larger supplies of body-building fish, such as white fish and herrings. The public were reminded such food was rich in protein, like meat. A number of cooking methods and recipes were suggested.

LAST POST COLLECTION TIMES

There was a feeling from some Suttonians of "bring back the Yanks". Complaints were made that local people were disturbed "by excessive noise from the British Army Post Office" that had taken over from the American Forces Post Office in Sutton Park. The B.A.P.O. "lorries were travelling along in convoys day and night". A councillor was quoted as saying "The noise of the Americans was sweet music compared with this!" Postal delays in Sutton were taken up by the local M.P., Sir John Mellor, with the Assistant Postmaster General. The latest collection times for first or second delivery next day from main Sutton Post Office were:

Location	Deliveries	
	First	Second
London, Head District Offices	8p.m.	
London Sub Districts	7p.m.	
Plymouth	2.30p.m.	7p.m.
Cardiff	6p.m.	11.30p.m.
Manchester	8.15p.m.	
Newcastle-on-Tyne	5.15p.m.	8.45p.m.
Edinburgh	5.30p.m.	7.30p.m.

A useful facility lost to many communities in more recent years is the local area collection, 4.30a.m., with a promised first delivery on that day. I was grateful for such a service on many occasions, taking urgent mail to the top of Mill Street around midnight or just after.

SEVEN YEAR OLD DELEGATED AUTHORITY

Linda Hunt's seven year old daughter felt very important when her chimney sweep father gave the child authority to sign the Duke Street school's account as paid, on receipt of the payment from the Headmistress, Miss Davis. During the summer months when the number of domestic chimneys required attention was low, Mr Hunt was pleased to give the annual service to the Odeon and Empress Cinemas. Linda recalled it really "helped with the cash flow".

With preparations going ahead for the state control of hospitals, Laura Cook was appreciative of the home confinement care given by Doctors Brown and Humphries with Nurse Smith of Elms Road. Mrs Cook received "very good

Fashion followers will note Mr Gilbert's record of the Baptist Church could be some years later than 1947. (Sutton Coldfield Library, George Gilbert, Dr. John Raines)

treatment at the Cottage Hospital for later major surgery and other members of the family". From memory Laura spoke in particular of "Miss Harrison who was the Matron and Nurse Mrs Benson. There were eight beds in the women's and men's wards and about ten for children. Each patient was attended by their own doctor". A survey was made of Good Hope to make it a Hospital with one hundred beds. The chairman of the Sutton Coldfield Hospital Management Committee advised there would need to be "considerable expenditure on the purchase and installation of new X-Ray equipment".

DISPENSARY DOWNTURN

The 1888 founded Sutton Coldfield Provident Dispensary, the services of which were often promoted by the Holy Trinity Church (end of Rectory Road), suffered from the planned 1948 National Health Service. The 58th Annual Report (for 1946) noted a fall in membership and funds "The close advent of the Government's health proposals has, no doubt, affected the situation". Membership dropped 1,114 to 1,642, with payments down from £1,322.15.10d. to £1,231.2.11d. Prescriptions dispensed fell by 1,378 to 12,523. Church collections rose from £265.15.11d. to £303.0.0d. Of the 11 major donation sources in 1946, the Warwickshire County Cinematography Fund raised £100, the Alexandra Rose Day £65, Sutton Municipal Charities £21 and Sutton Congregational Church £6.1.2d.

AMERICAN GIRLS ENVIOUS

In a happier mood, Sutton Coldfield Cricket Club celebrated its centenary with matches against Bromsgrove, B.V.G.S. and the Warwickshire Imps. In the later centenary weeks, a B.V.G.S. side with four masters in the team, only lost by seven runs to the host club. Such was the quality of the "'boys keen fielding skills, especially clean picking up and throwing in to wicket keeper and bowler". Sutton Coldfield C.C.C. considered the B.V.G.S. team as an invaluable "nursery" for future potential players.

The amenities available to students at the Sutton Coldfield High School for Girls, according to Miss Eileen McKenna, a Birmingham Council House staff member, "would make even High School girls in America envious". The "fine buildings and excellent educational amenities" were not matched in the U.S.A.

The summer of 1947 was a high point for many potential sea faring Sutton young men with the launching of T.S. Indomitable, a few hundred yards from the Boldmere Gate of Sutton Park. From the site an 80' longship was constructed to provide a fo'castle main-deck and ward room. Another alternative for boys who fancied themselves in a uniform was the Banners Gate Boys Brigade, formed in 1947.

PREDICTED END OF THE WIRELESS

A Sutton Councillor's forecast that the future end for ardent radio listeners was on the horizon caused anxiety to some in the Royal Town and amusement to others. This serious prediction came about when the Council approved plans for the construction of a Television B.B.C. Transmitting station, to be built on a site between Hillwood Common Road and Lichfield Road. The twenty-six acres would contain a one-storey building housing technical equipment plus the erection of a seven hundred and fifty foot high T.V. mast. The B.B.C. warned the area "would become sterile". Having the station within the Town would be an acquisition, with Sutton having its own special feature almost like a second Eiffel Tower. The pro-television lobby commented "ordinary radio and wireless would become out of date, superceded by television", another feature of modern progress.

BREAKFAST BEFORE 8.00a.m.

Conserving coal featured in a number of ways. Nationally the Government ordered train services to be cut by 10% compared with trains that ran in the summer of 1946. Passengers were encouraged by the Government "to travel mid-week if you can". Housewives were targeted again, being told to cook breakfast before 8.00a.m. or after 9.00a.m. If the ladies did that and delayed preparing other hot meals until after 6.00p.m., it "would go a long way to a further 25% reduction by domestic users" and they were further urged to accomplish this by the Birmingham Electric Supply Committee. Carters found illegally saving coal by giving short weight and over charging were fined. Alexander Comley Ltd. at the L.M.S. station wharf could help customers keep warm in the winter by burning unrationed peat blocks, while they were available in the summer. Stocks of these blocks could then be obtained and used as supplementary winter fuel.

One July evening many local and Sutton Park visitors found relaxation at Blackroot Pool, sitting or strolling past the anchored Bandstand listening to an enjoyable programme by the Clarion Singers. A record crowd participated in the Canwell Show that had a full programme introducing a great selection, all in sunshine. There was a record demand by leisure seekers, borrowing 531,868 books,

Demolition of buildings in preparation for the Model Falcon Lodge Estate.
(Sutton Coldfield Library, George Gilbert, Dr. Raines)

the highest in the history of the Town's Public Library since it began in March 1937. From the small stock provided at the newly instituted book service at the two hospitals, chiefly lighter literature was available. W.V.S. organised a valued book repair service, 1,143 volumes returned to circulation. 716 volumes were received from the public in response to an appeal to donate books to supplement the hospitals' limited budget.

BUS STATION - NOT YET

It was not "an opportune moment", so the Council decided not to go ahead with Sutton Bus Station, though it was noted nationalisation of transport was a few months away. Sutton's Mayor went on a trial run, with other dignitaries from the West Midlands on a new Midland 'Red', underfloored engined bus to Tenbury Wells. The Mayor found "it was the most comfortable bus they had travelled on". They were informed that 500 were being built, all on a 30' long streamlined design.

The report on the first post war game of Sutton Town in September, which they lost 1-3 at Brereton, advised News readers the local favourites lacked pre-match training. However, in their first home game at Coles Lane, they beat Stourbridge Reserves 2-1.

Six new subjects were offered in the 1947/8 programme by the School of Art and twenty eight different crafts and subjects within the wider Technical and Commercial Institute based in Lichfield Road.

1947 HONEYMOON

About her wedding in October 1947, Mrs Patricia Price told me, her "going away dress was my one extravagance - a pale green suit purchased from Rackhams for sixteen pounds!" The Wedding Breakfast was held at the Yenton Hotel, Wylde Green, where we enjoyed a three course meal with coffee at 8/6d. per head and the wine bill was £9.11.6d". They went by train for their Blackpool honeymoon. Pat added "it was not very glamorous compared to today's exotic destinations, but it must be remembered that in 1947 most seaside places still had barbed wire on the beaches and, in any event, in those times seaside resorts in winter were closed up and desolate". There were, however, perks for the newlyweds". At least in Blackpool there were theatres and shops and considerable activity, although the illuminations had not restarted since the beginning of the war". They enjoyed the "late October weather, the theatres and dancing at the Tower. Our happiness was complete. We had survived the war with its long separations and its austerity. Our dreams for the time being had all come true".

POST-HONEYMOON RATIONING

Food rationing continued for many years after the War. Pat remembered each person had 1/10d. worth of meat, 4 oz. margarine, 2 oz. of tea, 1 egg, etc. Pat came face-to-face with unlabelled paper bags that contained loose products. She was "proud of a delicious looking cake - until taking a few bites. We found our mouths beginning to shrivel. Instead of baking powder, she had mistakenly used alum. Another cake, with ingredients from an unlabelled paper bag, which she took to be ginger "contained pepper". Pat confessed "I was mortified by own own inadequacy until I discovered that an aunt had given her poor child not a Fenning's Cooling Powder, but a Bob Martin's dog powder instead". Pat and hubby managed. "Soap & sugar

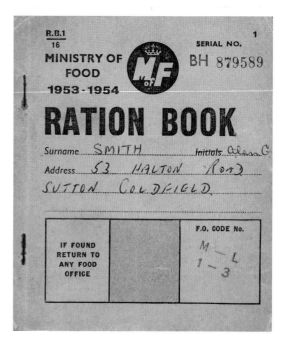

As Mrs Price mentioned, Ration Books were still around in 1953-54. (Alan Smith)

were rationed. We had to queue for practically everything, joining a queue without even asking what we were queueing for!" One wonders if the Royal Wedding couple had to do much queueing.

Sutton Council encouraged couples whose families had moved on, to take smaller corporation properties, so releasing scarce housing stock for young families, many with parents who were service personnel. The Council pushed the Minister of Health for resources to enable the Falcon Lodge Estate roads and sewers to be finished.

The Head Postmaster was reluctant to close Wylde Green Post Office. There had been no applications from two adverts.

Mr J. A. Dowdeswell retired in December 1947 as the Four Oaks Stationmaster. He remembered a bomb being dropped on a Four Oaks Station platform and parapet of the Lichfield Road (A38) railway bridge on 25th August 1940. Mr Dowdeswell had been on the railways including the L.M.S. for forty eight years. Other local L.M.S. Stationmasters at the time were: Mr F. Rogers at Sutton Coldfield and Mr Bestwick at Shenstone.

NEW MUM'S TWO WEEKS, OAKHURST CARE

"The moment I had my first inkling that I might be pregnant" Mrs Robbins wrote, "I went straight to Oakhurst, Anchorage Road to book myself in. This was just prior to N.H.S, we had to pay a fee." The experienced and knowledgeable midwifery staff, "laughed at me and said 'come back in a month or so when you are sure!' But I was sure." Dr. Hayward was their G.P., but Oakhurst provided pre-natal care. Just over nine months after the wedding her eldest daughter was born. Joyce "loved it in Oakhurst. There was good food, with seven days bed rest, then a longed for bath." The babies were brought to their mothers for feeding, then the mums were encouraged to stay in bed for the first week. The second week in Oakhurst included instructions on caring for the baby and managing home with the new arrival. When the nurse brought the babies to the mothers for feeding, "she would swing through the ward door, two tightly swaddled babies under each arm, handing them out to the appropriate mothers."

1947 TOP OF THE POPS

John Platt considered the 1947 Top of the Pops were: "Among My Souvenirs", "Come Back to Sorrento", "Now is the Hour" and "Maybe it's because I'm a Londoner".

Some issues concerning Suttonians in 1948 included: Sutton doctors and dentists held opposing views on the N.H.S.; the use of Sutton Park as a training ground for Olympic hopefuls; crisis year for farmers; British Rail nationalisation; fall back on "bully"; Sutton Coldfield's best residential areas; changes in X-ray staffing; Methodism arrives in Boldmere; the collection of Anderson and Morrison air raid shelters; and a B.B.C. drawn security curtain over Midland T.V.

Chapter Five

1948 – NHS ARRIVES, DISPENSARY DEPARTS

Alongside the development of private and council housing in Sutton, a Councillor, on behalf of servicemen and women, expressed gratitude to the Town Council's Housing Committee in expediting homes for those that had served abroad in the Forces. A private house was priced in Britwell Road, fetching £2,975, comprising 3 bedrooms, bathroom, lounge, breakfast room/kitchen, garage and gardens. A superior freehold property overlooking Sutton Park, a few minutes walk from the Parade, was £6,750. Accommodation included: 6 bedrooms, central heating, a two-car garage, excellent domestic arrangements, tennis court etc. Roadworks were proceeding on five private roads and "two other private roads, were not forgotten by long suffering people".

LOCAL DOCTORS BACK NHS

At a Meeting of Sutton Coldfield and area Doctors held at the Cottage Hospital, "they passed a unanimous resolution endorsing the B.M.A.'s approval of the National Health Service". Looking towards the staffing of the N.H.S., the Medical Officer of Health at the Council House, King Edward Square, advertised for the Sutton Coldfield Home Help Service. Women were required for "full-time employment, with a guaranteed weekly wage, with travelling expenses paid". Medical Staff with other members of the general public needing a taxi in the Borough had a choice of vehicles: 17 Austins; 6 Armstrong-Siddeleys; 2 Humbers; 2 Vauxhalls; 1 Rover and 1 Morris. Cab operators were named as: Harold Brighton of Highbridge Road; Ernest Clarke of Boldmere; John Joiner of Penns Lane; Eric Philips of Four Oaks; and Sydney Palmer of Jerome Road, amongst others. A Sutton commercial traveller was fined £3 for using petrol for a purpose other than that stated on the coupons. Instead of using the fuel for his work, he visited friends for meals. It was the first case under the control of Fuel Order, 1947, in the Borough.

THE EFFECTS OF INFLATION

The Sutton Coldfield News Leader highlighted "the upward sweep of wage-earners' incomes during the past five years". The article recommended that, "people should co-operate with Government to minimise the distressing effects of

George Gilbert, (assisted by Dr. Raines), encapsulated the familiar frontages of Slatter Dann, George Mason, John Frost and Chamberlains. (Sutton Coldfield Library, George Gilbert, Dr. John Raines.)

inflation". It was difficult to recruit bus drivers and conductors in the Sutton and North Birmingham because of higher factory wages. The Midland 'Red' second Staff Hostel was located at Vesey Road with accommodation for thirty employees. The full residential provision included meals and lounge with housekeeper living in and in full charge. Land was available to cultivate fresh vegetables and fruit for busmen's meals.

The need or desire for more money was expressed in a question at the Town Forum, broadcast by the B.B.C. Midlands Home Service from Sutton's Town Hall. Sir. Barry Jackson, Director of Birmingham Repertory Theatre gave his opinion on a subject topical in the third millennium. He "could not understand why this country was so 'dead set', against them. Personally he was in favour of state lotteries".

Hastilows 'Tudor Rose' coaches had their spring and summer inclusive holidays, promoted by Broads Travel Agency enticing people to purchase a summer holiday, in the cold weather, for eight days, at Morecambe and The Lakes, £11/11/-d and only £10/10/-d in North Wales.

SUTTON PARK OLYMPICS TRAINING

The amenities of Sutton Park were in demand by three groups in March 1948. The Town Council granted permission to the Oldbury and District Cycling Club to use a certain area of the Park on Sunday mornings between 6.00 a.m. and 8.30 a.m., in preparation for the Olympics. Adequate provision of marshalls by the Cycling Club was assured. The Club was told that the Council "would like to give them encouragement in their Olympic preparations". There would be benefits to Sutton in allowing the Sutton Coldfield branch of the National Farmers' Union to shoot pigeons on three Saturdays, supervised "by the Park Forester". The third group were required to "confine the flying of model aircraft" to the specified area near the Banners Gate entrance.

CINEMA WELFARE

An extension of the School monitoring system worked well at the New Cinema Club for Children at the Empress. Relief manager 'Uncle Sid' Perkins informed a reporter "many adult audiences were not as quiet or well-behaved". The Cinema Club elected forty-seven older members as "bosses", supervising outside queues and the audience inside the theatre. 'Welfare' monitors watched out for children feeling unwell, or taken ill at the Cinema. Each member had a birthday card and a complimentary seat for the next matinee. I rather rashly nominated Gwen in our road, already an elected "Boss", to sing a solo during a morning programme! The request fell on deaf ears, and the Girls' High School pupil was let off the hook. The Odeon's Club had similar objectives, apart from making money, to encourage children to get the 'cinema bug', to go to the Cinema's adult programmes in later years, or persuade parents or older siblings to take them. The Sutton Odeon appointed the first Cinema Padre in the district. Seven hundred children welcomed the Rev. Ronald Hirst, the local Baptist Church Minister. The Cinema Manager was quoted as saying "the Padre has the right approach to rising generations in their leisure hours".

LOOSENING OF THE PURSE-STRINGS

Local people were advised by the National Savings movement that folk "had forgotten prosperity and security had only been half won". The National Savings Committee spoke of a "loosening of the purse-strings and letting up on savings". The advert emphasised, "savings are an indispensable weapon in the battle for production on which our nation's future depends". A considerable amount of money was to be invested in converting Penns Hall into a residential hotel. It was pointed out the new hotel was 1,033 yards from the Fox Inn, Walmley, the nearest licenced premises. It was not intended "to attract the same type of Customer frequenting the 'Fox'". Mrs Done who, as a child, lived at the Fox, went with Dad to the Penns Hall auctions in 1948. Amongst "many items" he bought, was a Grand Piano – a beautiful Erard.

COLOSSAL FOOD LOSSES

Some Rotary Club Members may not have felt too well after lunch when they heard what had caused a colossal food loss, such as mastitis, abortion and infertility amongst cows. Luncheon guests heard that the ravages of Liver Fluke had caused the annual loss of 1,500 tons of bovine liver. T.B. also caused immense loss in meat.

LOCAL FARMING AFTER WORLD WAR II

"There were several family farms on the outskirts of Sutton", a farmer who wishes to remain anonymous told me. In 1945, he continued, "horses were still common on most farms doing light work, carting, harrowing, etc., although some farms still ploughed with horses". The family farms often hand-milked their few cows and had a milk round, either pony and float or an old car or van. "Milk was sold from a churn, with a ladle to fill up customers' jugs, or bottles with cardboard tops". The contributor added, "this was before tubercular testing and new hygiene regulations killed it off". Most medium-sized farms of two hundred acres or so were mixed farms. On them could be found "a dairy, corn, pigs, potatoes, sometimes sheep, etc. and hens". The food for the cows and other livestock was mostly grown on the farm. These included "rootcrops, i.e. mangels, swedes, kale, etc., fed to cows and mixed with oats and hay". The root crops the farmer felt "were very labour-intensive needing to be hoed and singled by hand. Everything was done by hand". My contact recalled "the Combine Harvester first appeared from the U.S.A. during the War. Tractors replaced horses, pulling ploughs, carts and other implements" soon after the War. The gradual mechanisation revolution resulted in many of the old traditional skills dying out. Rick building, both hay and corn; thatching ricks, etc. There was also the demise of the threshing machine driven by steam traction engine and usually owned by a contractor who went round farms mainly in winter, which was very labour-intensive.

ALL THE FUN OF THE FAIR

Although Pat Collins "had died at the end of 1943", according to Ned Williams, it was claimed in late March, 1948 the selection and quality of activities in Pat Collins' Sutton Park Amusement Park and pleasure gardens were on the same level as his four seaside locations that season. The Crystal Palace site was open daily. Prospective punters were promised "Super rides, including Giant Scenic Railway, Deluxe Dodgems, Flying Airways, Galloping Horses, Scooter Cars and the 1907 miniature Railway". Pat's adopted son, John, told Suttonians there was no need to go to Blackpool, Margate, Skegness or Great Yarmouth for entertainment – everything was available in Sutton Park, as well as new shows, exhibitions, cafes, music and dancing. A Crystal Palace "novelty" which, however, did create a bit of a rumpus in later years was "the fat woman". Apparently the interest in "the little man, had disappeared from British Fairs".

Mr Pat Collins - Brought fun, enjoyment and entertainment to thousands of visitors to the Crystal Palace Site - He died in 1943. (Ned Williams)

WOMEN IN THE LORDS

The News did not record if local women's Organisations voiced their disgust at Pat Collins' "fat woman", but they petitioned for women to be admitted to the House of Lords, on the same conditions as men. There were also demands for more women's toilets in the Borough. In particular at Boldmere and Beggars Bush. There was considerable debate as to why bread was still being rationed in 1948, three years after the end of the War!

Sutton Rugby Football Club returned in a happy mood from a successful West Country Easter Tour victorious over Budleigh Salterton and Withycombe. The latter in front of a crowd of several hundred.

There was considerable rejoicing on the Tower Road Estate with the first Post-War opening of twelve new bungalows for aged persons, provided by Sutton Corporation. The Mayor, A. Lucas, and his wife officiated at the opening ceremony.

CHAMBERLAINS FROM UNUSUAL ANGLE

Vacancies were offered at Foley Road, Streetly for a gardener, two days a week, a Sutton Engineering Company advertised for girl engineers, and an office needed a shorthand-typist on a five-day week. Chamberlains, on the Parade, required an experienced fish salesman and blockman.

Mr Dennis recalled an adventure with his young mates. They investigated the water routes under the Parade Shopping Centre. It seems their desire to explore the hidden world was taken on the spur of the moment because they wore their usual boots. Emerging from the dripping wet and caustic aromas of the Ebrook Culvert they were confronted by large amounts of debris adjacent to Chamberlains above. The excitement of the adventure soon wore off, when parents were seriously "upset" by the state of the pioneers' footwear and potentially dangerous escapade. John Dennis did not record if unwanted portions of fish from the Chamberlains' blockman were part of the debris the culvert warriors waded through.

BACK STREET THEATRE

There was not too much contact between Jerome Road and Ebrook Road families in general, though for folk with gardens adjoining there was some chatting and tolerance. There would also be some mixing of the children at school. One Ebrook Road group of teenagers encouraged contact, on one occasion, with children and youths from nearby roads at a price! I think it was during the long summer holidays the Ebrook Road young people at the Upper Holland Road end decided they could use their thespian skills to entertain other kids in the neighbourhood, supplementing their pocket-money into the bargain, through modest admission charges. Probably in the minds of the Ebrook Road Grammar and High School fraternity, some of the lower-rank and file Jerome Road riff-raff, certainly including Bassett, would benefit from out-of-school additional curricular activities.

Paying my sixpence, which was a lot of money, I joined a crowd of children and younger teenagers in a back garden. Evidently the home-made advertising of this unique venture had paid off, as the rather large subdued audience waited. The front of house and overall manager appeared to be Jeff Salter. After the welcome, the play went on. As the Tom Sawyer story was unravelled, many of the avid readers amongst us quickly identified the characters, anticipating scenes from the book. In general, the overall story was reasonably authentic with skillful improvisation within the available limited space and material. It was not easy to clap or encourage youths from a rival (at times) group, but they did on that occasion deserve it. If what seemed to be a successful event was repeated I cannot recall being aware of it.

PUBLIC'S PHOTOGRAPHIC CHOICE

Two innovations at the Sutton Coldfield's Photographic Society's ninth annual exhibition appeared to be successful. In addition to introducing a class for colour prints, reflecting an interest in that format, every visitor was invited to state on a ballot paper, their choice of the best picture exhibited. The public's selection of John Frost's 'Cotswold Hamlet', was not even commended by the Judges. It is important to remind the experts at times that the public's perception of what they enjoy and will pay for can be very different to the professional artist and judge. Or was the choice made because they knew and respected the local businessman?

NOT READY FOR N.H.S.

Some members of the public, having read the local doctors' "unanimous resolution to back the B.M.A.'s approval of the National Health Service", were taken aback by Sutton's other major professional team of health care providers, the dentists, who made a different decision. 13 dentists according to the News, "were not prepared to enter the N.H.S. in its present form", two months before its introduction. The local Dentists told the N.H.S. Managers the "present scheme was not in the best interests of patients". The named dental surgeons were: C.F. Apperson, E.W. Barrett, W.D. Clayton, N.G Evans, A. Germany, J.L.W. Gregory, C. Holme-Barnett, G.H. MacKenzie, V.D. Mash, B.O.M. Norris, J.A. Scott, W.A. Stockwin and G.H. Teall.

WHITEHOUSE COMMON BULLY

At the time of writing in 2003, bullying is regularly reported by the media, mainly at school or college, but sometimes at work and in the forces. With hindsight back in 1948, aged 13, I was probably an ideal target for the school bully. Only 5'6", not good at defending myself, naive on worldly issues, few friends, no big brother, really someone ready to be bullied by a Whitehouse Common hardnut. He regularly came to me in the playground with his minders, regaling me with disgusting stories of activities in his family. Cocooned in the protection of a small warm family home I knew nothing of such behaviour, though I would often appear to believe him. To argue or criticise him otherwise could have meant physical punishment away from the eyes of staff.

One day he and his cronies were having a 'bad day' in the playground. Seeing me gave them the opportunity to enjoy a laugh at my expense. He took, I think, my left arm and began to turn it into peculiar shapes – much to the mob's delight. Seeing how his supporters gained pleasure from his brave acts he pulled my arm over his back, with the excruciating pain the arm went limp. Returning to Victoria Road Boys' School some weeks later, with the broken arm healed, apparently I was to blame for fooling around!

PREVENTATIVE MEDICINE UNIT

Having improved the early detection capabilities amongst factory workers in Coventry and other Warwickshire towns, the mass Radiography Unit visited the Slipper Bath in South Parade. The main idea of the Unit's visit was to pick up early symptoms of pulmonary T.B., which enabled patients to have a higher chance of being cured. Former Jerome Road resident, Margaret Wilkins, reminded me of a lurking disease that teenagers in our road, including myself, could have caught by fool-hardy actions. Across from Mrs Crockett's Shop the Ebrook ran by the side of the recently erected new £600 fenced Sutton Town F.C. ground and the Holland Road playing fields, before skirting the Midland 'Red' bus garage and under Chamberlains. Between the Holland Road playing fields and the end of the football field fencing, Margaret remembered, "if the weather was nice and warm a crowd of local lads would dam the brook in Ebrook Road so that they could swim in it. Hardly healthy by today's rules considering that there was some sort of highly questionable outfall into the water just by the bridge. I dread to think what it was. However, we all survived". With other youngsters and youths I splashed about in the three foot or so deep water. It was a popular spot. Though our parents and older siblings warned us against the risk of polio, we individually thought "it will never happen to me!" Danger to public health concerned many Sutton folk because of a litter epidemic "mainly by one-day picnickers" in Sutton Park. The staffing in the Park had been: June 1938 – 48 men; June 1939 – 62 men; but in March 1948 – down to 37 men. The record Whit Monday Park attendance of 73,320 left less litter, though there were many broken bottles.

R.A.F. – DISGUSTING AND DISGRACEFUL BEHAVIOUR

The generally excellent relationships between R.A.F. 216 M.U. and the Town went into decline for a while. Seven Aircraftmen from the Whitehouse Common Depot caused drink and unlawful wounding offences in the Parade area. The defendants were told that it was the "most disgusting and disgraceful conduct without parallel recorded in the history of the Sutton Magistrates Court". The seven were imprisoned for seven days, two of the servicemen were regulars.

Sutton Coldfield was chosen to have the Midlands first new electricity showroom since nationalisation on 1st April, located in Vesey Buildings. The showrooms displayed "latest British made electric cookers, washing-machines, trouser presses, refrigerators, clocks and kettles".

BOLDMERE BROTHERHOOD – BOLDMERE METHODIST CHURCH

Mrs Britain and Alan Smith informed me of the 1911 formed Boldmere Brotherhood, held in the Boldmere Hall, and its combined significant contributions to the life of Boldmere and District up to 1948. From an outline history, in April of that year, "because of decreasing membership of the Boldmere Movement, it had been found advisable to call a Meeting to explore the suggestion of joining the Methodist Church". As the two organisations had some similar principles it was moved, "that the Boldmere Hall be made available to the Sutton Methodist Circuit for the purpose of conducting religious and social activities and that after a period, when legal and other matters had been cleared up, the whole work and building be handed over in their entirety". The first Methodist Service was held in September 1948.

Boldmere in good hands, Civil Defence personnel at the rear of Boldmere Hotel. Highbridge Road Fish and Chip proprietor Sid Cooling is last on the right of the back row. The lady on the extreme right is Nora Matthews.
(Alan Smith, Alick G. Wheeler)

Alan Smith told me "that in the late 1940's came the end of the A.R.P." His father joined the Civil Defence, which itself was short-lived".

SCOUT GROUPS IN THE SUTTON DISTRICT

Alan Smith, Chairman of the Sutton Coldfield West District Council, identified twelve Scout Groups in the Sutton area after the War. Eight were Church-sponsored Groups. The remaining four were at Highbridge Road, Princess Alice Orphanage, Duay Road and the Sutton Coldfield Sea Scouts in the Park.

NATIONALISED BUSES?

The nationalisation of British Railways became confused in some Newsreaders' minds with a similar policy for the Midland 'Red'. A reporter clarified for readers that although "some buses carry notices that they run in association with British Railways, 'their' users have been led to think, mistakenly that passenger buses have been nationalised, too". The journalist records the statement made on 1st January, 1948 by the newly formed B.R. "The fact that bus fares have not gone up ought to correct the false impression". A small steamline in the Town that did not attract nationalisation, though it became profitable, was the S.M.R..

SUTTON MINIATURE RAILWAY

John G. Tidmarsh, author of 'The Sutton Coldfield Fifteen Inch Gauge Railway', Plateway Press, 1990, writes that it "was one of the earliest 15" gauge lines in the country, though it began life in 1907, when laid down in Sutton, by the famous W. J. Bassett-Lowke as a 10¼" system". Re-gauging was in 1907/8. Mr Tidmarsh wrote "The line was approximately 1,000ft in length and ran in an almost straight line parallel to the Park boundary from the Crystal Palace to Wyndley Park Gate. The only major engineering feature was a bridge of some 30ft in length over a stream". The original route is shown in the Old Ordnance Survey Maps of Sutton Coldfield 1913 – The Godfrey Edition. In addition to the 1907 line, the two Midland Railway Stations at Sutton Park and Sutton Town, both with staggered platforms, are identified".

The S.M.R. became derelict from the early 1920's – 1938. John noted that the original Bassett-Lowke 4-4-2 steam locomotive, 'Mighty Atom', had moved round the country during these years, returning to Sutton in 1938 from the Great Yarmouth Minature Railway, as 'Prince of Wales', together with three closed bogie coaches, each holding twelve passengers.

Removal of L.N.W.R. turntable on the 1862 site at Sutton Coldfield Station - August 1937. (Roberts Family Collection)

In 1938 the arrival of equipment from Great Yarmouth Miniature Railway to Sutton, rejuvenated the line, it included a locomotive and coaching stock. (Arthur Spencer)

The Old Bassett-Lowke line at Sutton, seen in the 1913 map, Godfrey Edition, "still extant, was incorporated into a completely new and lengthened layout, laid down for Showman Pat Collins by Mr Parkinson Senior from the Great Yarmouth Railway, in early 1938. The total journey distance was approximately three thousand feet, making a large balloon, from the covered terminus, which also acted as engine and carriage shed, and contained a platform road and an engine release loop".

John Tidmarsh recalled that Black Country businessman Tom Hunt bought the SMR, "in 1948 from Collins in a very run-down condition". Mr Hunt acquired a new 4-4-2 locomotive from a private railway at Tewkesbury – this, John informed me became "No.1 'Sutton Belle' and was built in 1933". Other parts from Tewkesbury eventually made a similar loco, which Mr Hunt completed in 1952 as No.2 'Sutton Flyer'.

MAGNIFICENT FAIRGROUND ORGAN

It was in 1948 that John Tidmarsh became aware of another great attraction at the Crystal Palace fairground. "The Dragon and Peacock Scenic Ride – eight large

The 98 key Marenghi -style instrument with Wonderland No. 2 Bioscope showfront at Crystal Palace in 1948. (John Tidmarsh)

gondola-type cars with dragon or peacock heads and tails, which travelled under a canvas roof (tilt) and a magnificent fairground organ in the middle – the origins of which dated back to 1908". John continued "the show front was built by the famous French firm of Marenghi and Cie" and was supplied, together with a very large organ for a Bioscope Show, (forerunner of the cinema).

John recalled that "Pat Collins had two bioscopes and the Sutton Showfront came from the Wonderland No.2 bioscope. The original organ – a 98 key Marenghi – was heavily rebuilt in the 1940's by the London firm of Messrs. V. Chiappa and its first appearance after overhaul was at the Aston Onion Fair in 1948, after which it went to Hull Fair and from there to Sutton". Its usual operator John described as "a wiry, wizened, little man, George Corbett, who, like the fairground Manager big Billy Bagnall, lived in an immaculate and comfortable showman's caravan on site".

Favourite Past-Time - Countless children have fed the Wyndley Pool ducks. A rather nice pose is displayed on the left. The Sutton Coldfield Miniature Railway was nearby. (Arthur Adderley)

AGRICULTURAL EXPANSION PROGRAMME

The Government encouraged farmers to increase and expand their productivity by recruiting more permanent rather than part-time or seasonal labour. My father, Albert, was a full-time cowman for Mr Frank Cattell at the Falcon Lodge Farm. In addition to milking and caring for the cows, he worked with the horses in the fields, being an all-round experienced farm worker, conversant with most types of farm activities whatever the season. However, my impression was that he was not particularly well paid, but as mentioned earlier, fresh milk, vegetables, sometimes meat and eggs all helped Mom balance the housekeeping budget.

Sutton's butchers in 1948 sometimes had smaller size Sunday joints, which needed "sixpenceworth" of 'bully' to equal the amount of carcass meat. In July eggs were plentiful in some shops. A dozen cost 1/6d in one shop, but 2/6d in another. Perhaps they were different sizes! My brother, David, remembered that Mr Humpherson at 3, Jerome Road had a pigsty and shed for hens. The families that gave him pigswill were rewarded with some bacon at least once a year, often near Christmas.

START OF THE N.H.S.

On 5th July, the Birmingham Regional Hospital Board's Group No.23 comprised eight hospitals and two clinics, according to the News, providing medical services for the Sutton Coldfield, Tamworth and Lichfield areas. After thirty-four years of valuable work, the Sutton Coldfield Maternity and Child Welfare Committee ceased to exist. It was stated in the final report that the Committee provided an efficient, progressive Home Help Service. Considering the needs of Post-War Sutton, the Committee recommended the putting up of "communal laundries on housing estates". These would assist families with the "shortage of soap, hardness of water, saving fuel, in comparative small kitchens to work in". Such laundries would be much appreciated by estate tenants, "without placing an extra heavy burden on the rates". The cost of vital services in the town had risen sharply after the War. Ambulance and Fire Brigade provision in late 1930's set back the Sutton authority under £2,000. The 1948 figure payable to Warwickshire C.C. was £12,000. "Sutton was considered 'a very rich town'". It was alleged, "Sutton Coldfield was helping to pay for services in other County districts where there are now services far better than ever before".

Princess Alice Orphanage College at New Oscott gave value for money in their two year full-time Child Care Course. Initially twenty-three students were enrolled on the Course, however, two withdrew owing to illness, one transferred to a teacher training Course, and the remaining twenty men and women qualified with a final Child Care Certificate. Of these, four students were from abroad. One wonders if any former P.A.O. children decided to take up a career in child care?

TOWN NEEDED R.A.F. SITE

Irritation by the Town Council over the Air Ministry's continued tenancy of the Whitehouse Common site was forcefully expressed in July. The Council's objections centred on the proposal to use the R.A.F. site as a suitable location for light industrial development, as that type of land was "extremely limited in the Borough". The closeness of the Falcon Lodge Estate, it was stated, could "provide convenient and suitable housing accommodation". It appeared the Council "anticipated that the Air Ministry tenancy would be temporary, ending with cessation of hostilities". Sceptics may have thought the recent prison sentences of seven R.A.F. airmen from 216 M.U. indicated to the Council, that service personnel had overstayed their welcome. With hindsight the relinquishing of the lease of most of the site by Military tenants had almost another five decades to run! The primary sewer and drain facilities for the first two hundred of the planned sixteen hundred Falcon Lodge Estate properties had been started.

Sutton's Mayor, "condemned large school classes". At the Burcot Grange High School, Four Oaks, Annual prize distribution, the Mayor advocated "there must always be a personal link, relationship between the teacher and the child". The School Principal informed the audience "There is no doubt that the school has progressed well". There was still little news about the Moat House Estate's sale, however there was talk of the building of a County College and Technical Institute.

NEW AIR SERVICE

An Airspeed "Consul" aircraft of Patrick-Duval Aviation Ltd took off from Elmdon Airport on 16th July, being the first internal scheduled service operated by a private Company since the end of the War. P.D.A. was an associate of B.E.A. The four times weekly service went to the Isle-of-Man with connections to Dublin and Glasgow.

Even going via the Isle-of-Man to Dublin would be much quicker than by train and ferry for business people in Sutton Coldfield.

RATIONING CHANGES

How influential was the demand by women's organisations four months earlier to finish bread rationing, because the Government stopped it on 24th July, 1948? Local bakers told a News reporter, the only difference was the speeding up of the service, with no longer the need to cut out bread units. Mr A. Stokes of 20, Birmingham Road "had to stipulate cake for regular customers only and not to casual buyers". On the last day, however, there had been a rush with spare bread units for flour. Miss R. Latham, Manageress at Bennetts on the Parade, "had seen one small advantage with rationing. It minimised bread wastage". The 1948 national harvesting would have over 6,000 Combine Harvesters to cope. Various tips on making the most effective 'use of a Combine Harvester' were given in the News, so the material for 1948/49 bread making could be gathered in successfully.

A new scale of Clothing coupon rates was introduced. There remained, however, some items being in short supply, some plentiful. "A major shortage was all types of outside fittings in women's clothing and moderately priced night wear". The manageress of E. & R. Wilkes, on the Birmingham Road, commented "if Coupon rationing was removed, it would mean an increase in demand for some lines. Essential things in short demand were still being imported".

"RATION THEM NOW!"

Going against the national dislike of rationing, some Sutton shopkeepers "called for a form of rationing because of a shortage caused by women". A cross-section of tobacconists favoured cigarette rationing. One of the reasons for rationing was that "too many women had started smoking during the War". The News reported that queues formed rapidly with rumours "of cigs expected in shops". Generally queues were quiet and orderly.

MOLLY BADHAM'S RECOLLECTIONS

Molly Badham, referring to her days at the Sutton Pet Show before Hints and Twycross Zoo, wrote: "Remembering back to the days of the Pet Shop in Station Street, there was a wine shop on one side and a Saddlers – Shaws – on the other". Miss Badham continued, "I also remember Evans the Butchers, Georges (Roses) Greengrocers and Liptons on the Parade". My own wife, Joan, when she worked at Boots, supplied Miss Badham with regular supplies of nappy wear for the famous T.V. Chimps. The Badhams 'brought delight' to thousands of children and adults, with the selection of pets available from their shop. The Chimps were always a topic of conversation in the Pet Shop and their amusing T.V. commercial antics made them stars to many local children in the 1950's.

NEW WALMLEY ACTIVITIES

John Pritchard recollected, "there was little for boys to do in Walmley", so a Meeting to consider some profitable activity in the village received much interest. Gathering in the Village Hall parents and lads responded to the invitation from the Vicar of St. John's, Rev. W.A. Weeks, and Church Organist, David Holt. It became clear from the Meeting some constructive pursuits for the boys was essential. However, some parents thought the activities should be scout-based and not the start of Boy Brigade sessions. Disappointed, some boys did not join the successful Boys Brigade's Lifeboy Group. Mr Pritchard mentioned the Boy's Brigade Company at Banners Gate 'were a tremendous help in the early Walmley years'. Apparently the "majority of the Walmley members were also in St. John's Choir".

MIKE'S MOST SUCCESSFUL SEASON

Over in Boldmere, St. Michael's F.C. enjoyed their "most successful season", although they lost in the F.A. Amateur Cup Semi-Final, 2-0 against Barnet before 27,000 at Highbury, Arsenal's ground. That was quite an achievement to reach this stage, also reaching the Semi-Final stage of the F.A.Junior Cup, though losing 4-2 to Old Selecians in Essex. They missed winning the Central Amateur League Championship by a narrow margin. Four other St. Mike's sides gave impressive accounts of themselves in the 1947-48 season. The team's Directors wanted the ground made secure, preventing children causing damage to the pitch. Sutton Council advised the Club "the ground must be open", whereas the Town ground was enclosed. The quality of the Boldmere Team, considered internationally, was evident when they were selected to host a game against the Indian Olympic F.C. 'The Mike's' impressed the visitors, though losing 1-0.

B.B.C. T.V. TRANSMITTER STATION BEGUN

Six months into its construction programme, Hill's Vicar, Rev. G.B. White, petitioned that the Sutton Coldfield B.B.C. Transmitter Station Mast should be called the Hill T.V. Mast, reflecting its location, as one of the highest points in Warwickshire. Competition between T.V. dealers was expected to exceed T.V. Set supply. Anticipating the demand, R.F. Sweeney opened another Branch. With some

Birmingham T.V. dealers having, "long waiting lists for sets", the B.B.C. drew a "security curtain over Midland T.V., until arrangements were more advanced". An earlier Councillor's prophecy that T.V. would be the end of the wireless seemed likely to be fulfiled. Estimates of the England and Wales population were around forty-three and a half million at the time, and it was estimated that Sutton's catchment area would reach six million viewers.

RAILWAY TRESPASSING

Two Jerome Road male residents landed up in the Sutton Magistrates Court, fined thirty shillings each for fighting and being bound over to keep the peace for twelve months. It seems the assault case developed from three boys trespassing on the railway bank, and then throwing stones at Jerome Road properties opposite. It was a great temptation to kids, including myself, to play on the railway bank, walk along the railway lines, and sometimes cross the two running lines going down the other bank to the Coleshill Road recreation ground to play football or just muck around. Against parental admonishing, most of us put caution to the wind and, foolishly, putting ourselves and others at risk from fatal or serious injury from passing trains. Our greatest crime as teenagers was probably taking junior school-age children over the heavily graded line, where the youngsters may not have been fast enough to avoid being struck by fast moving trains. We were reported to the authorities, with the police seeking out the culprits. Generally the Council Estate people 'kept mum,' but they told the kid's parents, with some children getting a hiding or, at least, a severe ticking off.

MILLIONAIRE CHAUFFEUR

Sunday afternoons 'us scallywags' gathered outside a widow's house, thirty yards from my home. We must have looked a right sight, old clothing, some ripped, a number wearing hand-me-downs, and nondescript footwear. Probably, though we did not notice at the time, we let off disturbing aromas. On reflection, many decades later it is incredible that such an activity could have taken place on a Sutton Council Estate road, but it certainly did. I was one of the participants on many occasions. There would be a cheer from the children as they identified the gleaming beautiful Bentley effortlessly gliding down Jerome Road from the Royal Road direction, and past the house with the pigsty. Somehow, we got into some kind of line as the car stopped and Councillor Alfred Owen, later Sir Alfred Owen, got out and called at Mrs Gilbert's with the weekly rent for the widow of one of his respected New Hall Staff.

New Hall with Moat - The owner of New Hall gave children from a council estate rides in his Bentley. They queued up in anticipation of a ride. (David Owen, O.B.E.)

Even in the presence of such an important, influential businessman and local politician we squabbled and pushed each other to get a comfortable position on the luxuriously upholstered leather rear seat. Mr Owen called at Mrs Gilbert's on his way home from leading a Boy's Crusader Class at the Parade premises, which John Tidmarsh, amongst others, attended. His son, David, now the Chairman of Rubery Owen Holdings Ltd, wrote that, "I well remember too the visits to Mrs Gilbert and the crowds that gathered for a 'ride'". Once our friendly millionaire's polite chauffeur was satisfied we all had a seat, off we went down the road, past the two shops, right into Ebrook Road, speeding up Upper Holland Road, right past the King's Arms, smoothly into Royal Road for another sixty miles per hour burst of speed, arriving in Jerome Road at a more sedate pace. With excited thanks we left the perspired covered leather work and life once more became as normal. On the Owen's way home to tea, a call was made to leave rent with Mrs Swainson, another New Hall widow. Did our Bentley driver ever get caught going over the speed limit?

ANGLING FOR LOCAL INTEREST

Sutton Coldfield Angling Society, the first for fishermen in the locality, was formed in 1948, demonstrating the growing number of organisations formed for various interests. The Society leased a stretch of the River Anker, just outside Tamworth. Foxhill Pool at Little Sutton, was to be restocked. James Pool, identified by the German Air Force in October, 1939, was also to benefit from a restocking programme. The Society cautiously qualified the restocking, "maybe some time before any fish will be caught". Not far from James Pool, seventeen-year-old John Pritchett of Rectory Road was the 1948 Boys' Amateur Golf Champion. Having left BVGS, John started his career as a golfer on the Kilmarnock Course, Barassie in Ayrshire.

PROVIDENT DISPENSARY CLOSED

As forecast for some time with the introduction of the N.H.S., the 1888 founded Sutton Coldfield Provident Dispensary closed on July 5th, 1948 after nearly sixty years service, in particular attending to the needs of Sutton's working classes. The Mayor, ALD. J.B. Stone, laid the foundation stone on 27th June, 1888. At the end of the first year 1,279 persons attended the dispensary, receiving medical attention, medicines etc. At the end of 1911 memberships had grown to 3,070, though it fell to 2,771 when the National Health Insurance Act was implemented. The highest membership between the Wars was 2,072 in 1936. At the close of 1946 it was down to 1,642. The remaining assets to be transferred to trustees of the Municipal Charities. At the last meeting, Mr J. Ellison, was the only person present who had been connected with the service since it began. Some of the medical people associated with the Dispensary were: Drs. Chavasse; Jerome; Knott and Sir. Alfred Evans.

NEW COMMUNITY INITIATIVES

Local preacher, John Edwards, the Secretary of the Sutton Coldfield Baptist Church, "paid tribute to those who cared for the Church in the past". Church members joined in a thanksgiving weekend at the paying off of the six hundred and fifty pound debt. I later met that dignified family man at Duke Street Hall. His request to some youth leaders at that Hall changed my career plan in 1957.

Sutton Coldfield Congregational Church bought a house in Bishops Road as a manse for their new Minister, the Rev. T.J. Lander. Janice Moore said, "it cost three thousand, five hundred pounds".

Mr Lander introduced a number of initiatives for the good of the community. Councillor A.G.B. Owen shared with Britwell Men's Circle he "believed religion did mix with business". At least he told the members "it operated at Rubery Owen", where he was a Director. Dr. Harper attended the Boldmere Children's Church. For him it became an obsession to collect a stamp each Sunday to be fixed in the collector's book. "Canon Brown was a very friendly, helpful Vicar", Dr. Harper commented.

DEVELOPMENT OF X-RAY FACILITIES

In October 1948, the first task for former R.A.M.C. Radiographer, Dennis Wilkinson was to visit all the Group 23 Hospitals with the Group's Secretary, Mr A. G. Till. As the Group's new Radiographer, in charge of the Department, he covered "Sutton Cottage, Victoria Hospital, Lichfield; St. Michael's Hospital, Lichfield; Hammerwich Hospital; General Hospital, Tamworth; St. Edith's Hospital, Tamworth and Bolehall Hospital, Tamworth". During that Sunday they established what sort of X-Ray equipment, if any, they had and what it was capable of doing". The Cottage was the "only one already being run with good equipment, trained staff and Dr. Cecil Teall, a Birmingham Consultant Radiologist who lived in Sutton, coming in to report on films". St. Michael's at Lichfield was the "administration centre for the Hospital Group, though the X-Ray Services were run from Sutton".

SELF-TAUGHT STAFF

At the Lichfield Victoria and Tamworth General X-Ray Departments "the Radiographs were taken by Matron or Assistant Matron or the requesting G.P.". Mr Wilkinson found the resultant X-Rays by the 'self-taught' health professions, "sometimes left much to be desired". The catchment area also included "Brownhills, Chase Terrace, Chasetown, Burntwood, and also a small Hospital for babies at Canwell". From the start of the "new Service to the Group of Hospitals", Dennis initially travelled between hospitals with X-Ray equipment already installed at the four locations at Sutton, Victoria, Lichfield, Hammerwich and Tamworth General, one morning at one, the afternoon in another. The Radiographer recalled that the catchment area near to "Hammerwich was larger than that of Lichfield, yet this had the smallest facility and a very 'portable' X-Ray set". As the Hospitals in Group 23 were run by "local G.P.'s, there was not much 'out of hours' work done". As far as Mr Wilkinson remembers, "there was no resident medical staff at any of the Hospitals". Further improvements from the start made in 1948 were seen in 1949.

THE COLD WAR

Going through local newspapers and listening to local people's memories, topics of wider interest surfaced, some with international ramifications. Sutton's M.P., Sir. John Mellor, brought such a matter before his constituency. He alleged Russia, "was playing Hitler's game – the old game of dictatorship versus democracy". He considered the U.K. came out losers in the share of information between the two countries. The M.P. had evidence that, "we – the U.K. - were letting them know too much. The Russians did not let us know anything!".

NATIONAL HEALTH DRUGS

A Family Forum at Mere Green on the National Health Act, heard Dr. John Amos field a question on the availability and cost of drugs under the new scheme. He reassured the audience that there "were ample stocks of drugs for any emergency and there was no danger of a shortage arising". For Suttonians anxious about the cost of drugs the doctor was adamant in those early days of the N.H.S., "Drugs were supplied regardless of cost". In central Sutton, the Committee of the Homes of Rest, stated "that as it did not come under the New Health Act" the charity was in "greater need for more subscriptions and increased donations", to keep that vital work operational.

SUTTON'S BEST RESIDENTIAL AREAS

November saw the announcement of the Ministry of Town and Country Planning's West Midlands plan, Sutton's annual expansion had risen to one thousand, four hundred and fifty housing units, which meant an additional three hundred and eighty houses each year for fourteen years. Mr Tom Porter, the Borough Surveyor, informed the Town "there is plenty of land to build on – but there should be provision of suitable industries". Perhaps an echo of give us back the R.A.F. base! Mr Porter claimed that Sutton had "become a most desirable residential town". In the Borough surveyor's opinion in 1948, the "best residential areas were: a) east of Birmingham Road beginning in Wylde Green – continuing up into the Town Centre; b) then in an arc north-west over Four Oaks and Streetly to the Chester Road". Between the Wars "Sutton, Solihull, and Aldridge led the expansion of Birmingham's suburbs". Under the re-distribution of population, the Ministry required Sutton "to take an extra twelve thousand by 1962 over and above the normal expected increase of eight thousand". If that happened, the population of Sutton Coldfield's Borough would be nearly sixty-six thousand by 1962.

MOAT HOUSE SALE

Warwickshire Education Committee paid twelve thousand, three hundred pounds for the Moat House. The new site to be called, 'Sutton Coldfield College of Further Education' with added new technical and commercial departments. A new College Room could hold five hundred students and two hundred and forty County College Students a day. They anticipated a demand for day and evening classes.

It was also anticipated two-thirds of Sutton shoppers at Christmas 1948 "will be able to get a turkey", though there was concern over the black market in English birds. However, 'Sutton', according to the News of December 18, "was specially favoured with goose or boiling fowl available for those without a turkey." The difficulties of food rationing were again apparent with a Coles Lane Grocer baffling shoppers with similar descriptions of commodities. He sold Beef Steak and Kidney as well as Beefsteak and Kidney pudding. He retained coupons of the higher value. That Christmas-time the Court fined him ten pounds. He may have found consolation by listening to one of the five Top of the Pops in 1948, chosen by John Platt, years later. They were: 'Nature Boy', 'Galway Bay', 'Slow Boat to China', 'You can't be True Dear' and 'A Tree in the Meadow'.

1949 was to be the year, when B.B.C. Television programmes would be transmitted from the new Hilltop Television Station, overlooking much of Warwickshire and Staffordshire.

Chapter Six

1949 – SUTTON'S NEW NATIONAL IDENTITY

SUTTON HOSPITAL'S BED SHORTAGE

Early N.H.S. difficulties over Sutton bed availability was reported in January, 1949. Yet the News was told by an N.H.S. spokesman, "If a G.P. wants a bed for an aged person today he stands a better chance of getting one than he did twelve months ago". The story that caused a flap was that emergency beds were being offered at two Birmingham Hospitals because the fifty-four beds in Sutton Cottage and Good Hope Annexe were already occupied. Another Hospital statement acknowledged there was insufficient provisions. A future N.H.S. 800-bed hospital on Chester Road was materialising on the drawing board.

Another potential shortage was pointed out by an N.F.U. representative at their Annual Dinner. Mr R.W.N. Dawe spoke of "The danger of taking over agricultural land for building purposes and cutting down home food production as a result". The Mayor, Cllr. C.H. Dainty, referred to the "dilemma facing local authorities". There are more than two thousand people waiting for houses in Sutton. Thinking of the developing Falcon Lodge Estate, he continued, "what were once fields and quiet lanes will soon be a forest of houses. Personally I do not like it, but what are we to do? People need these houses, the whole building problem is a tragedy". A few weeks later, when the Mayor and Cllr. A.G.B. Owen, the Housing Committee Chairmen, were at the opening of the first four houses in a F.L.E. block, Cllr. Owen announced, "many people would thank the Council for developing this estate. The work started from two ends". It was the Housing Committee's Chairman's hope that, when developed the estate would be Sutton Coldfield's Garden Village". A F.L.E. bus service was to start shortly.

TELEVISION TRANSMISSION STATION DELAYED

In late January, 1949, the Sutton Coldfield B.B.C. Transmitting Station's opening was delayed until the end of November, 1949. It was noted in the News that experts abbreviated television to 'Tee Vee'. Some enthusiastic T.V. followers from Sutton visited a special display of mobile television equipment in Birmingham and were televised for their trouble.

NOT PROPER BEEF SAUSAGES

Beef sausages made the papers in February. Sutton magistrates fined a Boldmere butcher for selling the sausages with less than 50% meat. The analysis certificate showed they only contained 32.6%. The local butcher and an Aston butcher, who were prosecuted together, pleaded that they did not manufacture the sausages. However, they were both fined four pounds with eight shillings costs. A long-standing company keeping the right side of the law was Davenport and Co, advertising their fifty years of service, claiming to be "Sutton's leading coal merchants, having been founded in 1899 and selling coke, logs, and anthracite in addition to coal from the Park Station Wharf." Over at Blackroot Pool, six steel paddle-boats at thirty-five pounds each were being purchased in the Spring, for the children's play area.

Pat Collins Fun Fair, Easter Monday, 1949. The Fair operated by Pat's adopted son John, was obviously having a good day. The big dipper is on the left. The Crystal Palace is in the background. The three rides from the right are: Moon Rocket; Waltzer; Tilt-A-Whirl; with the Dragon and Peacock scenic ride, nearest to the Crystal Palace. (John Tidmarsh)

POSTMAN'S 230,000 MILES

A Postman who delivered mail in Erdington and Sutton from 1906, retired in March having traipsed two hundred and thirty thousand miles on the local rounds. In the early days, he recalled, "the entire day's mail for Erdington and Sutton Coldfield was brought in one horse-drawn van from Birmingham". Another local man, known for his slick footwork, ran the touch line at the televised 1948/49 F.A. Cup Final at Wembley (Wolves v. Leicester City). Mr R.L. Aldridge of Four Oaks was a well known sportsman around Sutton, refereeing local Charity games.

An R.A.F. 216 M.U. Airman sold for £11.10shillings in London, some of the six thousand five hundred cigarettes he had stolen from a break in on Rectory Road newsagents and tobacconists. The man was committed for trial at Warwick Quarter Sessions.

QUALITY SCHOOL DINNERS

Chairman of Sutton's Welfare Committee, the Mayor, advised the Council that there had been increases in the number of dinners, milk, and meals served to children each week compared with 1948. Councillor C.H. Dainty said, "he had not seen such quality and quantity in ten years". He emphasised, "No other children in the Midlands were having better food cooked and served", after visits to the Boldmere and Tile Cross Kitchens. The estimated number of meals in 1949-50 was five hundred and sixty-eight thousand. Presumably the school children noted and tasted the "Quality and Quantity" of the food.

With the lifting of lighting restrictions in April, members of the A.B.C. Minor's Club at the Empress Cinema saw the brilliantly lit cinema front, which was turned on by the Manager. Two shops in a 'blaze of light' were a millinery shop and a dry cleaners. In the following weeks more premises were brightly lit in the town.

AIR AND BUS SERVICES

The gradual development of air-services from regional airports also continued at Elmdon with a thrice-weekly departure to Paris, using a twenty-one seater Douglas Dakota D.C.3 Aircraft. It left Birmingham at 9.45 a.m. for the one-hundred-and-twenty-five minute flight. The eighteen pounds return fare included a connection car service at New Street Railway Station.

Some Boldmere residents voiced their anger at West Bromwich buses running through the village on the 25 route without picking up passengers. They were annoyed to learn the Banners Gate – Parade fare was the same as the through West Bromwich

– Sutton one. The Midland 'Red' fares over the same route should be charged. Boldmere folk found the 107 Midland 'Red' services, particularly in the summer, were packed with visitors to the Park, so Boldmere people were left behind. W.B.C. Transport department decided they would not reduce their Boldmere area fare.

END OF SWEET RATIONING, OR IS IT?

The end of rationing was a big day in the majority of children's lives and potential business for Sutton's dentists, with private and N.H.S. patients. Within a month, the News spoke of rumours circulating in the town "That sweets will have to be put back on rations, because there were insufficient supplies to go round". Outside one sweetshop two signboards showed alongside each other a 'No Cigarettes" notice to adults with a 'No Sweets' sign bringing, disappointment and disbelief to young customers. Contacting the Ministry of Food, the News Reporter said the Ministry denied there was a sweet shortage. People were buying too much!

Sydney Eyles, Dispensing and Photographic Chemists of Sutton Coldfield High Street, advertised the reintroduction of a Pre-War Service to Sutton customers. The 'First Post-War, twenty-four hours Developing and Printing Service for films in Sutton could be offered, except at peak periods.

JEROME ROVERS

I came up with a solution enabling me to get a regular game of football. Owing to my lack of skills on the pitch, whatever I said in conversations to others, no local managers or captains wanted me. Though I played for Victoria Road Boys' School Team twice! The answer to getting no football opportunities was by organising and managing my own team at 15, plus sending in written reports to the News on losses under 6-0. Yet, quite frequently we still won by more than ten goals. Being the manager, coach etc., I was, of course, responsible for team selection. Without any qualms, I put myself in

Jerome Road residents and friends. Perhaps Rover Supporters? (Miss Dolphin)

as inside right. My inadequacy was forcefully brought to my attention during a game when I shot towards the goal. One member I heard say to another forward, "It's the first time I've ever seen him hit a ball hard". It's amazing how older players were prepared to put up with me, but fortunately for me they did, and overall we did enjoy ourselves. However, some unsporting actions against me did happen. Behind my back they must have had many laughs at my expense! I expect the News Sport Reporters spent some hours making sense of my contributions!

BILLY BARLOW AND GEORGE HUMPHERSON JNR.

A number of Jerome Road lads played for The Rovers, and two are mentioned in an early report published in May, 1949. The Rovers beat Maney Celtic 2-0. "Billy Barlow", who lived across the road, was complimented on "playing well and scoring from fifteen yards". George Humpherson Junior, the pig-keeper's son, "kept goal well for the Rovers". With humility the report praised, "Fletcher making good saves for Maney". I presume the original writer was saying the Rovers deserved a bigger victory! My pocket money did not allow me to negotiate contracts for the Rover players. This led to a disturbing situation. On a number of occasions some of my older, disaffected players arranged games under the name of Jerome Rovers without my knowledge, which they lost, sending in reports to the News. It used to rile me for a while. I later decided it was a back-handed compliment!

PESTERING PAID-OFF

Continuing John Tidmarsh's fascination with the Sutton Miniature Railway, "one day in 1949 a friend of mine, Michael Phillips from Boldmere Drive, another K.E.G.S Aston pupil and I pestered the driver Jim Glover for a job so much that he put us onto breaking up coal and filling the tender – I suppose he thought that this would cure us (or our mothers would forbid any further visits because we got so black!)". Jim Glover, and the lads' mothers were in for a shock if they anticipated John and Michael would be disillusioned from working at the dirty, but practical end of miniature railway operations. With a sense of satisfaction John enlightened me. "However, quite the opposite happened, and it opened the door to a new world – association with the little railway quickly developed and it became my principal spare-time activity right through until going up to University in 1955 – and beyond, during University vacations, and led to a life-long love for miniature railways". Thinking of his career he found the S.M.R., "a wonderful basic training in railway engineering, operation and maintenance – and in human relations and teamwork. A good preparation for my subsequent career with British Railways".

No. 1 'Sutton Belle' leaving the station with a three coach train. The de-sheeted open coaches suggest a busy day. (Bernard R. Haynes)

John Tidmarsh considered this as "a nice action shot on the curve past Wyndley Pool, about halfway round the circuit". 'Sutton Belle' is probably driven by Jim Glover, around 1954-56 (Bernard R. Haynes)

A VERY SPECIAL MAN

That was Mr Tidmarsh's description of the S.M.R. owner, Tom Hunt. "Mr Hunt was a Black Country industrialist with a son, Bill, the same age as myself. He was a warm-hearted man and treated Michael and me with great kindness and generosity. He encouraged us in our growing love of little trains". As a further encouragement to John and Michael and in appreciation for their voluntary assistance, he took them and all the staff of the S.M.R. on "an outing to the Talyllyn Railway in Wales each year".

Dr. Harper, a former pupil of Green Lane Primary School remembered someone with special qualities. To him, Miss Townrow was "excellent" at the school, with Miss Freeman as the Headmistress, and Miss Skelton teaching the 4-5 year olds. Mr Elliott, had the top form in a separate building across the road, and, as a pupil, found the lattice metal footbridge "ideal for train spotting". He recalled the signals for the Chester Road goods yard were controlled from the station. He also remembered Horace's Greengrocery Shop on the corner of Green Lane and Little Green Lane. "Goods were delivered in Horace's motorised 3-wheeler van".

1949 MARRIAGE

Comparing the 1947 weddings of Patricia Price and Joyce Robbins with those of 1949 showed things remained difficult for couples marrying in 1949. Ray Showell, "had been in constant touch throughout his time in the Pacific, serving with Destroyer Command of the British Pacific Fleet, with Romola". Returning to the U.K. in 1946 they were engaged in 1947. Romola was at a teachers' training college in Bingley, Yorkshire. As soon as he could, "I travelled up to see her – nothing I had experienced in the Pacific was as terrifying as venturing into an all female college!".

In his recollections of Sutton after W.W.II he found the Round Table and Rotary were very active. During his "time in Round Table we were involved in projects at Watson House (a children's home) and Princess Alice Orphanage". Thinking back to the "East Coast floods of that period saw Round Table organising a lorry-load of relief items – the lorry provided by a local trader with goods supplied and collected in Sutton".

FAMILY RALLIED AROUND

Similar to the two weddings two years before, for Romola and Ray, "rationing was still in force, food, clothing, furniture etc." Even so Ray considered, "we seemed to

Lord Rowallan getting out of a Sutton Sea Scout Boat during his brief visit to Sutton Park in 1949. (Sutton Sea Scouts, Alan Smith)

Lord Rowallan with local Sea Scouts in 1949. Did the visit to the beautiful Sutton Park influence the choice of a world event location in 1957? (Sutton Sea Scouts, Alan Smith)

do exceedingly well". That was in no small way due to the "family that rallied around, coupons and vouchers appeared and we were able to furnish our first house in Wylde Green quite well". They were married at "St. Michael's Boldmere by Canon Brown and honeymooned in Minehead", rather than Blackpool in 1947.

NEWSPAPER DELIVERIES

Mrs Rose Cook assisted in the newsagents at the corner of Upper Clifton Road and Park Road. It developed in size over the years. The newspaper boys delivered as far away as Monmouth Drive and Lichfield Road. Two groups of customers were schoolboys, calling for sweets, and the Sutton Park Staff. Rose gave an insight into local people's relationships with Park personnel. The Chief Park Ranger lived in the property close to the main entrance. She also remembers Joe on the main gate. He kept an eye on local children, allowing them to play in the stream. When the parents came to the gate he took the children to the parents, "making sure they went from the Park with someone they knew and could trust". Apparently another Park Ranger was resident by the Banners Gate entrance.

PROPHETIC VISIT!

One wonders if Lord Rowallan's "flying visit of fifteen minutes to Sutton Park", in the Spring of 1949, when he was impressed by the facilities and location of the local Sea Scouts, had any influence on a later World event. National leaders of industry, commerce and youth movements, amongst other organisations, can note on paper, or in their memory something which is exceptional in its category that maybe of significant value or use to members at a later date. Even eight years later!

ALL CHANGE

Janice Moore, reflecting on the, "untiring work of their Pastor, the Church encouraged him to take a day off whenever possible. Their early appreciation of his leadership at the Park Road Congregational Church received from him, "thanks of all friends for the gift of an autocycle", a great asset in his pastoral work. The Church lighting was changed from D.C. to A.C. a move initiated by Mr Landor.

The St. John's Walmley Boy's Brigade members explored new ground with their first Annual Camp going to Abergele in North Wales. Over the years they visited many parts of England and Wales.

Scouter Alan Smith's memories of early holidays after the War, included members and children of the 1942 formed 67 Club which had three weeks under

First Camp at Abergele in 1949 for the 2nd Sutton Coldfield Boy's Brigade of St. John's Walmley, which was founded in 1948. (John Pritchard)

canvas, when the eleven families stayed at a Coleshill Farm. After the first week the dads went into work by bus to Birmingham for the remaining fortnight. The necessary equipment was taken by Clarke's Transport from Gate Lane, Boldmere.

The 67 Club went to Saundersfoot in Carmarthen Bay for two weeks. In those continuing days of rationing a Clark's Transport driver with "UC US everywhere" on the back doors, went some miles too far, delivering the group's camping gear, etc., at Saundersfoot. He was later fined by magistrates 'for being in an area', where Clark's were not licensed to be.

FURTHER BRANCH LIBRARY

With the opening of the new Walmley Branch Library, with three thousand volumes, it completed the first circle of branch libraries at Hill, Streetly and Boldmere. The Walmley Branch was in one half of a renovated army hut. The other half accommodating a maternity and welfare centre. It was acknowledged that other estates such as "Falcon Lodge, would be wanting branches in future".

News column writer 'Freres' questioned why no V.E. Day Anniversary Celebrations were arranged in 1949, including "local clubs started on the first

V.E. Day". Freres suggested the apparent lack of interest was because: a) there was a universal acceptance of uninterrupted peace; or b) merely a wish to forget the horrors of those black years.

Streetly Station Railway Porter, Mr A.E. Brooker, of Hill Hook Road, helped to produce a sense of peace at the station". One Streetly resident, sitting on a station platform seat, informed the News, "it is the quietest spot in the district". The passenger admitted the "colourfulness of flowers lining the station fence, had been created from the Porter's long hours tending the blooms, occasionally helped by Station Master, Mr E.J. Hankin".

HARVEST CAMPS FOR SCHOOL CHILDREN

Owing to the ongoing critical shortage of farm workers, for a second year running, the Ministries of Education and Agriculture combined to enable "older school children to assist in the gathering in of the Country's crops, especially the potato harvest". As far as I recall children like myself in the older sections of schools in Sutton Coldfield worked daily on a farm during the week. We were not in a residential harvest camp, probably because Dad worked at Mr Cattell's farm. I did my potato picking up there in view of the slowly emerging Falcon Lodge Estate. What I do remember is the excruciating back pain from the lengthy bending down and gathering up of the potatoes. Despite the moaning and working out in the heat, winds and rain, the realisation they were free from school and being paid into the

The preparation of the Springfield Road section of the Falcon Lodge Estate, with the farm in the background. (Birmingham Library Services)

bargain were sufficient daily motivators for 1940's teenagers.
HORSE-SENSE

My memory fortunately cares not to fully remember the background to the later part of my potato picking work. As far as I recall, I did not moan to dad about the hard work of potato picking, the way my sensitive hands were blistering, or my face not dealing well with the varied hot, cold, indifferent weather conditions out in the open. It may be in response to my mother's enquiries about how I was getting on – I was honest in my replies! Or I may have told my six-year-old younger brother, David, and he passed on the true picture. Whatever the circumstances, to my surprise the farm management decided I was not particularly suited to just potato picking. On reconsideration years later, their assessment was probably accurate. Though my father, after his time each morning in the dairy, came to work on the potato harvesting, I am not aware whether he was in charge or not. Obviously as a

Three children moved from Duke Street to 269 Springfield Road on the Falcon Estate in 1949. Their memories of the move, and later years on the Estate are included in the Fifties book. The photograph of Paul, Mary and Ted Roberts records them with the plaque commemorating the completion of the first houses on the Falcon Lodge Estate. (Mr Mrs Warner, Author)

member of the farm labour team, he would have some influence on which children did what. One day, working at my usual pace there may be a clue there – my father told the children, in the group I was a member of, that with my knowledge of horses at the farm I had been chosen to be section horse leader.

This strenuous and presumably intellectually demanding position also required good communicating skills with the duty horse. My dad usually teamed me up with the most docile beast. Some teenagers, Mr Cattell and other farming staff would have complimented dad for such good matching of horse and section leader. Whichever horse it was knew the procedure of going so far before being told when to stop and when to go. It was impressed upon me by dad and other staff, when he was not there, to give confident sharp, short, clear instructions to the horse. Gradually, "Wow, Jessica" or "Wow, Rocky", or whatever the name was, brought the animal to an abrupt halt. After too many incidents of the horse carrying on, and the teenagers swearing at me for my obvious incompetence, causing them to walk further with a basket of spuds to put on the trailer, the horses and I began to work together. As I enjoyed going home with a painless back, healthy hands and face, it seemed to me the farm had made the right choice of making me section horse leader. It certainly suited me!

COLES LANE BETTING HOUSE

An unsuspecting eleven-year-old boy was stopped by police in Coles Lane, as he went to a house they had under observation. The police found the boy had a betting slip with money, about to place a bet on behalf of adults. At a subsequent Court Hearing, three men and two women were each fined one pound, though it could have been up to one hundred pounds each. The Police Superintendent suggested to the Court, "That I think using the boy is the most deplorable thing about this case".

FOLEY ROAD D.I.Y. BUILDER

Encouraged by the local authority to construct your own property, presumably hiring architect, builders etc., a Foley Road potential builder went on a part-time course in the basic principles of bricklaying. Completing the course, he began at the site in 1946 with the bungalow being finished in 1949, including timber flooring throughout. In his spare time he had laid all the foundations, drains, concreting and used nearly twenty thousand bricks. His course at the Birmingham Technical Centre had paid dividends for him.

Frequent practice of the theory brought success at the first under sixteen-year olds Gymkhana, contested by one hundred and fifty entries. The competition was extremely keen. Philip Whalley gained the Silver Cup, Christine Holland won a set of irons in second place, with Sylvia Blankensee in third place being presented with a riding crop. The event organisers, themselves regular competitors at Pony Sports in the district, Valerie Hanman and Barbara Poole, decided to promote an "even bigger and better Show in 1950, but still limited to competitors not over sixteen-years old".

The preparations for the introduction of television within the Midlands involved T.V. Test Signals from the B.B.C. pilot transmitter at Frankley Beeches. "This proved fairly successful in Sutton Coldfield and District". The test picture was televised for dealers, three hours in the morning and three hours in the afternoon. The mobile transmitter was moved for further testing around Coventry and Wolverhampton. With pictures coming from the new seven hundred and fifty foot transmitter expected just before Christmas, the B.B.C. anticipated satisfactory reception up to one hundred miles away from Sutton. An attraction making its first Post-War visit to the locality in October, would be seen in people's homes many times in the future on the developing T.V. Network. Bertram Mills Circus took to the road in 1946, claiming to have "Britain's largest 'Big Top'", seating three thousand, five hundred people. Admission being between 2/6d – 12/6d, including

Sunday afternoon with Gran. It was expected that the children would be in their Sunday best. (Alan Smith)

Tax. The next tour stop after Sutton Coldfield was Leicester.

A LEARNING EXPERIENCE: PARDON!

The fourteen-year olds at Victoria Road Boys' School moved to the Technical College in Lichfield Road, next to Bishop Vesey's Grammar School, for their last year in education. We were treated more like students than schoolchildren, and probably responded in more constructive ways than with the Victoria Road Boys' School Headmaster. If pupils were not paying attention to him at the front, he would disappear and half-a-minute later, Mr Gregory would come behind the culprits banging their ears with his clenched hand. Regrettably my ears buzzed and throbbed a couple of times. The teacher/instructor appointed for the final year came from the Tamworth area. Seeking to widen job opportunities for us potential employees, he introduced us townies to a number of environments with which we were not familiar.

One of these environmental expeditions took us to Kingsbury, outside Tamworth. At intervals class-mates went out of sight, then amongst the last ones we were made to stand to attention, pressed together in a small rickety cage. Bells rang, safety bars re-checked, ill-fitting helmets at alarming tilts, then whoosh! Some maniac regulating our descent, really wanted to scare us to death. In years to come Drayton Manor white knuckle rides had nothing on this death-challenging experience. In the prolonged, yet rapid forty-five seconds my stomach seemed to be going in the opposite direction to my legs. Other party members with ashen faces waited to find out who had been sick, comparing experiences of the 'mad ride'. Even after viewing modern techniques of harvesting coal and hearing of the tempting wages, a collier's job was one that I would not tick on the Youth Employment Officer's form, early next year!

RADIOGRAPHY IMPROVEMENTS

Mr Wilkinson, as Group Superintendent Radiographer "saw several improvements, particularly with the addition of qualified radiographers to Sutton, Lichfield and Tamworth General, hospital's staff."

The first Radiologist was Dr. Charles Griffiths, who lived at Shenstone. "The need for an out-of-hours service was introduced for X-Rays. Dennis still recalled, "the sensational article in the Tamworth Herald stating, 'Man waits three hours in agony for an X-Ray'", An injured footballer was taken to Tamworth General Hospital, where he had to wait for the G.P. who had to attend to his surgery, see the man, then call Dennis out. "In those days", Dennis informed me, "I was living the other side of Birmingham with a journey of about twenty miles to Tamworth and I only had a Morris Minor". Once there, the man was quickly dealt with. In future months and years, improved X-Ray equipment was installed in Sutton, Victoria, General and St. Edith's Hospital, as well as Hammerwich. Gradually in later years more involved X Ray examinations were taken on and Dr. Griffiths was involved in doing Barium studies and other examinations which required an injection of dye. Mr Wilkinson recalled that a retired R.A.M.C. Surgeon, Mr Shepherd, was the first Sutton Cottage Hospital Surgeon also available to other hospitals.

STRONG COMMUNITY SPIRIT

Molly Daniels considered "Sutton had its own identity, with Mayor and strong community spirit". Amongst the local population she thought "many were grateful for the guidance and care shown to youngsters in those days by Club Leaders and Professional Artists, who took the trouble to become involved with us in those interesting days".

BIGGEST EVER LOCAL CAKE

W.H. Bromwich of Four Oaks baked, what was believed to be, the biggest cake in the locality, celebrating the then eightieth anniversary of the founding of the National Children's Homes. It had four tiers, the top one weighed one Cwt, being nine feet high, and five feet across, illuminated with eight electric lights. The cake was due to be cut at a Birmingham Town Hall party.

Another costly item was the New Refuse Destructor at eighteen thousand, four hundred and fifty-three pounds, opened by Councillor S.C. Brown, the Chairman of the Health Committee. The L.A.I.S. equipment, closed in November 1948, dealt with forty-five tons of refuse every twenty-four hours. The new one handled forty-eight tons in eight hours. It provided efficient and hygienic treatment of refuse involving the stages of handling, screening, salvage recovery and incineration.

PROBLEMS OF FOOD HYGIENE AND THE MIND

The Medical Officer of Health was heartened by over two thousand, six hundred people taking the trouble to visit the Sutton Health Exhibition. He commented, "we feel that there is an increasing interest in all aspects of food hygiene" from all the queries they had received. The exhibition committee "was pleased with the fine attendance by school children".

Doctors were accused of a lack of sensitivity at a local club. Mr Humphries shared their concerns with the local Soroptimists Society. To him, "There's not enough sensitivity in the minds of some doctors who ridicule the psychiatrist". He had noted, "the patience with which these men dealt with 'nervous' (battle shocked) troops in Military hospitals."

A couple familiar to many service people, Wilfred and Mabel Pickles, were at the Parade premises of W.H. Smith, where Wilfred signed copies of his latest book. They found Sutton a "very attractive" place. If they had to live around Birmingham, they were quite certain they would like to live in Sutton Coldfield. The couple found time to meet many people and roughly two hundred and fifty books were signed personally by him. Pamela Done remembered Wilfred Pickles being collected from New Street Station to take part in a broadcast from Boldmere.

The West Bromwich buses were stopping in Jockey Road, with sample fares - Beggars Bush to Jockey Road 3d, and to the South Parade Terminus - 4d.

TELEVISION SLOWLY ENDS - AUSTERITY AND SCARCITY

One of the two longest serving engineers at the Sutton T.V. Station Transmitter, travelled into the Borough from Birmingham, whilst it was being constructed. Looking back, Norman Green recalls the small number of road-users reflecting the limited number of car owners in the early Post-War period. Norman eventually lived not far from his work place. Mr Green wrote, "for television to come to the Midlands in 1949, only four years after the War, conveyed a feeling of the slow ending of austerity and scarcity resulting from the many ravages of the War". For the engineer, "The heart of the television station was the T.V. transmitter hall". Norman described it as a 'long hall with windows set high in the roof. At one end was the Vision Transmitter. This was a structure of gleaming grey steel cupboards about thirty feet long, seven feet high and seven feet in depth. It was packed with electric circuiting". Its function was to "produce the thirty-five kilowatts - later upgraded to fifty - of radio waves". These were passed up the mast and then transmitted from the aerial. Mr Green advised me, "at the other end of the hall was the sound transmitter, about sixteen feet long".

DECEMBER 17TH "ON THE AIR"

Moving on to 1949, he described that in the middle back of the hall were doors to the air intake ducting and vents from the roof. To cool the valves, large quantities of air had to be blown over them. Suffice to say, stressed Norman, "that the fan motors were about twenty horsepower each". Inside these air intake stacks were banks of air filters "originally like cotton wool between wire gauze". This was needed to catch the "soot and other impurities from the air in those days before smokeless

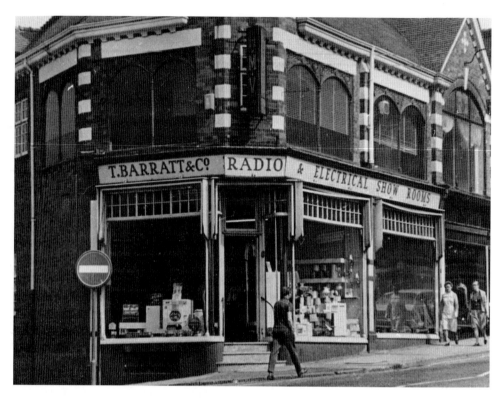

T. Barratt & Co. Mill Street Showrooms - The firm provided staff to assist the B.B.C. in preparation for T.V. transmission. (Ian Price)

zones stopped the burning of coal in domestic grates".

On Saturday 17th December, Sutton Coldfield's B.B.C. T.V. transmitter was "on the air". The four days 'Telly parade' Exhibition at the Orange Grove, marking the T.V. transmitter's opening had hundreds of people visiting. Mrs Patricia Price, 'whose father was Mr Thomas Barratt, founder of T. Barratt and Co said, "he was - to the forefront and the main T.V. supplier in the Sutton Coldfield area: also supplying engineers for work at the B.B.C. Television Station at Hill Village".

Mr Green told me, "Peter Hawkins and myself were the only engineers who saw the 405 line Sutton Coldfield transmission start, and remained to see them end. Everybody else had gone to other places". Eight years later Norman at the T.V. Station witnessed a storm commented upon world wide.

Chapter Seven

1950 – SUTTON'S DEEP DARK SECRET

T.V. WINNER

Mrs Swann was delighted to win a ninety-eight guineas Phillips Consol T.V. set in a competition. "She posted her entry at the very last minute". Looking into 1950 she pondered, "my darning will pile up!"

Warwickshire County Fire Service responded to the extremely difficult position of recruiting part-time firemen in Sutton Coldfield and Solihull by making both towns manned on a permanent full-time basis. It also recognised the growth and importance of the two areas, attracting working, middle and higher class residents.

Cinema entertainment at the beginning of 1950 at the Empress and Pavilion was Ronald Regan, Patricia Neal and Richard Todd in 'the Hasty Heart'. The Odeon offered, 'Captain from Castile', starring Tyrone Power, Jean Peters and Cesar Romero.

The B.B.C. thanked Sutton Town Council for "their hospitality over the opening of the T.V. transmitter". The Upper Holland Road Garages of the Midland 'Red' was extended on 31st January, to hold one hundred vehicles from the 1949 allocation of 73.

UTILITY RANGE OF CLOTHING

Sutton News 'speaking As Woman to Woman', columnist Winifred Hallam, considered the 1950 utility range of clothing was better than ever before. It enabled, "women of moderate means to dress smartly, economically, following a few simple rules". The basic colours "for your wardrobe – black, navy or brown" should be of 'simple lines', always avoiding fussy trimmings and too much detail. In Winifred's opinion the "most useful type of all – purpose coat, for the girl with a limited income is a full-length swagger, such as Diana Dors, star of 'Diamond City', wears". The ideal basic wardrobe would be "teaming up a plain suit, a light wear wool dress, and one of the short evening dresses; one can then ring the changes".

QUEEN STREET MYSTERY GAS EXPLOSION

At 5.30 a.m. Sunday morning, an explosion in a Queen Street house reminded some local people of an aerial bomb when detonated. The force was so strong a man was blown through a window across to the other side of the road. The house was severely wrecked. "2 dogs thought dead. A couple and two sons recovered".

The Orange Grove Ballroom was transformed from the old, cold, frigid glass and steelwork of the Old Crystal Palace "into a Winter wonderland garden effect. It effusively strikes a very cordial note".

The Midland 'Red' busses were fitted with suppressors eliminating the possibility of interference with T.V. reception.

Norman Green said, "within a month or two of operating, filters needed replacing at the T.V. Station. They became black and smelled strongly of soot".

NEW AMERICAN FAD – SLIMMING

The News Fashion Writer comments highlighted "young women at coffee bars, stylishly dressed, height of fashion, chattering, smoking, swinging their nylon sheathed legs doing everything except eat". Apparently, the fashion writer had decided, "Sutton and District's young women in 1950 had heard from magazines in America that it is fashionable to be slim". For our young women, "instead of a bite out of a chop or steak, you just sipped coffee, nibbled a biscuit, talked about matters of the heart, and so kept the pangs of hunger at bay". A Mother-figure person cautioned, "be sensible about dieting".

ENLARGED SUTTON COLDFIELD CONSTITUENCY

With a record turnout of an eighty-two per cent poll, Sir John Mellor (Conservative) won with 36,017 Votes, though Miss Audrey Wilson for Labour, increased the Socialist Vote to 21,364. Employment vacancies in the Conservative-held constituency were for a bread delivery man – experience being essential, post advertised by the Horne Royal Bakery. Young girls were being recruited for light, clean, interesting work, in the binding department of Saxton Printers Ltd in Newhall Street.

Emerging evangelist, Stephen Olford, spoke at Sutton's first Youth for Christ Rally in Sutton Town Hall. Community singing was led by Mr W.H. Day of Duke Street Hall, and assisted by the Ambassadors Male Voice Quartet.

1950 CENTRAL SUTTON FROM THE AIR

A 1950 Simmons Aerofilms Ltd photograph of central Sutton Coldfield records what part of the Royal Borough looked like towards the close of 'Sutton Coldfield In The Forties' survey of the town. To assist in identifying buildings and features a summary of the picture's content begins around Rectory Road.

Simmons Aerofilms Ltd.

CENTRAL SUTTON COLDFIELD - 1950

Towards the top of the picture can be seen the cemetery, with Rectory Road and the park on the right. The two staggered Midland Railway station buildings of Sutton Town are located down Midland Drive from Coleshill Street entrance. The Vesey Gardens are easily visible in front of the Parish Church.

Near the junction of Coleshill Road and Rectory Road can be seen the Royal British Legion building. To the right of Trinity Hill is the Rectory. At the bottom of Trinity Hill is the Girl's School on the left, and Victoria Road Boy's School on the right, facing Sutton Baptist Church, the site was later occupied by McDonalds. Across from the Dog Inn is the lower section of the parade, with the rear views of the top end of the Parade shops.

Tucked into the bottom left hand corner of the photograph is the congregational church in Park Road, now the Sutton Coldfield Gracechurch United Reformed Church. The former Barratt's electrical shop is on the Station Street corner, with the Telephone exchange to the left. Moving up Millstreet on the right is the former 1859 Town Hall, with the Post Office on the left with a number of buildings behind.

Moving down Midland Drive again is the wooded area behind the Birmingham side station building now occupied by a housing development.

SMALL SHOPS COULD DISAPPEAR

Sutton's Mayor, Councillor H. Hottersall, gave ominous predictions of the demise of Sutton's small shopkeepers, at the annual Dinner Dance of the Town's Chamber of Trade. The Mayor said, "I can foresee the time when small shops and individualists will disappear, and when the Regional Commissioners' canteen will be open on the Parade". He encouraged Suttonians to "shop in your own Royal Town". He saw buses full on Thursday afternoons – our half-day in Sutton, with people going shopping in Birmingham. "He thought they probably returned with goods which he was sure they could have purchased quite as reasonably, and with

Local Shop - R. J. Haynes draper, hosier and boot dealer at 42 Riland Road in 1950. The type of local shop the C-of-T thought could disappear. (Bernard R. Haynes)

greater convenience and comfort, in Sutton Coldfield". Local Chamber of Trade President, Mr A.H. Wright, said "the individual shop gave better service than any government-controlled undertaking, most people were realising this every day". The local C. of T. "will do all in their power to help with the 1951 Festival".

IN MR SHEPHERD'S HANDS

The school nurse looked into my hair at intervals, which with other children we accepted as part of school life. So a school visit by the doctor to all older pupils in the Autumn/Winter of 1949, was seen as something all teenage boys and girls were subjected to. After the medical the school doctor and my mother talked of treatment to correct a condition. The operation would be in Birmingham. At Mum's request, Mr Shepherd, our Sutton General Surgeon, agreed to operate on me at the local hospital. Presumably people told me what the treatment would be, but as a fourteen year old, it was a frightening experience.

Admitted the day before surgery, the nurses advised me that an enema would be administered to me by a male nurse that evening. Requests for information were stonewalled by, wait and see. The procedure was efficiently carried out with little discomfort, but it does now bring to mind a daffodil and a Colonel in a 1959 film. Having thanked the anaesthetist the next morning, and told to count to ten, a rubber mask was put over my face. Some unexpected perks came in the post-operative days in the hospital, with confectionery, books, visits, etc. However, I was distressed as I waited for my turn to go to theatre, to see hospital staff bringing younger children from the theatre back on Ward and picking them up by the hair! Some while later it was confirmed that Mr Shepherd's efforts on me had been successful, so I am grateful for his skills as Sutton's first General Surgeon.

MANY CLUBS IN DEBT

Mr L.W. Tingle, Hon. Treasurer of the British Legion (Sutton Coldfield) Club Ltd, reported it had a one hundred and three pounds deficiency, though all obligations were paid. Money had been invested in restoring the Club premises "to tip-top condition". 1950 looked more hopeful with fifty-five new members accepted recently, thereby increasing the membership to two hundred and seventy-one. Mr Tingle told members, "the same story of losses by Clubs was heard on every side". With pride, Walmley Social Club, at their sixteenth Annual Meeting, announced that a successful year had been enjoyed, keeping in profit. The membership was two hundred and forty-three". The Sutton Coldfield Corporation Loan debt rose from £1,225,918 in 1948/9 to £1,546,381 in 1949/50.

FOUR OAKS TOP STATION – FOR HOW LONG?

I wonder if I had noticed the Sutton News report on Four Oaks Railway Station being awarded the best kept Station competition trophy, with maximum points of five hundred for the garden and two hundred for general Station cleanliness, that I would have considered a Junior Porter's job there? All the major qualities and skills were foreign to me. A half of each day on the early 6 a.m. – 2.20 p.m. and 11.50 a.m. – 8.10 p.m. afternoon shifts required cleaning of the Station, plus preparing coal fires, lighting them, scrubbing and polishing ladies' waiting room/toilets, lino floors, washing out male toilets, cleaning brass work, then assisting the foreman in the gardens. However, helping passengers with timetable

Four Oaks Goods Checker and Station Master John Shallis. (Richard Coleman)

A 1949 view of the 1884 L.N.W.R. downside building at Four Oaks Station. (Eric Russell)

enquiries, recording parcels from Belper and Baldock, pushing barrows of Private Schoolchildren's luggage was manageable. At that time in March, my parents were getting concerned because I was apparently showing no interest in any type of employment. Mr John Shallis was a proud man, so was station foreman, Mr Alf Webb, the gardening king, having served at the Station for seventeen years. How long would their pride continue?

CONTACT LENS

Scrivens in Paradise Street, Birmingham, informed potential customers of "substantial reductions in the price of contact lenses". Sutton News readers learned that the "lens were worn under the eye lids, giving a wider field of vision". The promoters promised the lens "would be comfortable and could not be detected, thus allowing the eyes to retain their natural appearance".

The recently formed Sutton Coldfield Battery of Territorials was being prepared to receive national servicemen "in increasing numbers", after completing the statutory two years full-time service. The local T.A.'s new H.Q. was at Artillery House, 313 Birmingham Road, Wylde Green.

COAL SHORTAGE CONTINUES

Mr Green and colleagues were concerned about the high amount of soot in the air, affecting the T.V. mast transmissions, but Sutton Coldfield coal merchants endorsed the Minister of Fuel and Power, Mr P. Noel-Baker, "supplies are our great difficulty nowadays". The N.C.B. was unable to meet the merchants' demands. The main difficulty for the Minister and coal merchants, "is in the quality of the coal available". Most large coal was needed for the railways and export. The Minister admitted in the House, and what Mr Green probably suspected, "we have been obliged to allocate to merchants some coal of grades which would not be put to household use if there were adequate supplies of better coal". Defending the N.C.B., "the Minister emphasised they were not to blame for the great shortage of plant to wash and prepare the coal". Members of the Sutton Coldfield Housewives' League, however, were not letting the local coal merchants off the hook. The ladies were strongly advised by their reps that a "coal merchant can refuse to accept bad coal. They will be recompensed by the N.C.B.". It was impossible to say, the H.L. members were told, "when the situation will improve".

SIGNIFICANT EVENTS

A number of contributors had significant things occur in their lives in 1950. Olive wrote of leaving Princess Alice's Orphanage. "I was fostered with a couple who wanted a coloured child. My father was Sri Lankian and my mother was English and also a child who had no involved parents. At the time I was the one child that fitted the bill," she lived with them, "till I married". There was an unexpected outcome for the young woman. "I married my foster brother, whom I had never met till I was eighteen years old".

The Harper's first car, Dr. Harper thinks, "was in 1950. We had a Morris Minor, registration KNX 110". Somewhat later his parents "hired a car and driver to take the family to Barmouth".

When Elizabeth moved with her parents, on to the Falcon Lodge Estate, which became an award-design of Sutton Borough and Warwickshire County Councils, "Churchill Parade shops were not in existence". They lived in Newdigate Road.

Richard Shine was impressed by "the very good caring Dr. Dipple gave, who succeeded Dr. Amos". Alan Smith pointed out the life saving preventative procedures at Keeper's Pool. The efficient service given by Jim Hudson went almost unnoticed as he "rowed a rescue boat round the pool section at busy times". Fortunately for erring swimmers and others that found themselves in trouble, "Jim was a very keen and good swimmer".

BLACKROOT CONCERTS

The 1950 Concert season of visiting bands at Blackroot Pool saw a gradual increase in popularity of outdoor music being played to picnic crowds on the grass, whilst children played on the paddle boats in their separated section, close to the Concert pontoon. Mr Newbury wrote, "The Amington Band played in Sutton Park, probably twice in the season at Blackroot Pool. Various players played solos on cornet, euphonium and trombone. We had no vocalists". The Band went to the Park by coach. "The launch, which took people around the love pool, conveyed the band to the pontoon". It was probably the launch named 'Crusader'. One Sunday "two of the Band's thirteen year olds missed the Coach from the Tamworth area, but made their own way to the Concert. A helpful Park boatman took them to the pontoon, but the Conductor refused to have them on the pontoon, for being late". Mr Newbury remembered that "good size crowds listened, well-behaved and attentive". At each engagement they gave two programmes; in the afternoon at 3p.m and the evening from 7p.m. The band refreshed themselves at a local Café for afternoon tea between performances. Each performance included five items, followed by an interval and four further items. The band had a wide repertoire.

Blackroot Pool Summer Concerts - At a safe distance from the children's water area, the Amington band provide a summer Sunday relaxing concert. (G. Clarke)

Of the five marches in different programmes sent to me, they included: 'Cossack', 'On Tour', 'Elephant' and 'Pat in America'. The overtures were: 'Napoleon', 'Maritana', 'Pipue Dame', 'Crown Diamonds', 'La Overturia' and 'Barber of Seville'. Under musical comedy the band rendered the 'Desert Song', and 'The Girl on the Film'. Each complete performance finished with 'God Save the King'.

BUS SERVICES LESS AFFECTED BY CARS THAN TRAINS!

Folk attending the forty-fifth A.G.M. of the Midland 'Red' learned that, in the opinion of the directorate, "it was probably correct to say that private cars are far more competitive with railways than they are with buses". The spokesperson said, "it is certainly correct to say that the railways have a great deal more to fear from the competition of private cars than from the competition of buses".

Having passed my medical at Derby and an interview with Mr John Shallis, I began as a raw junior porter at Four Oaks, being required to clean the more substantial building on the down side to Lichfield. The first service to New Street was the 6.10 a.m. from Four Oaks. The light engine arrived in reasonable time to heat the empty, non-corridor, stock in the upside sidings. In the cold weather with the steam covering the bang-closed carriage door windows, at the bay platform it was a welcoming sight for our workmen passengers. Most tickets at that time of day were to Aston, Vauxhall and Duddeston, and of course, Birmingham. Passengers for the Midland line to Barnt Green and Redditch changed at New Street. The early workmen services developed from the 7.45 a.m. to business and executive passengers on 7.58, 8.18 and 8.28, and they were often crowded, particularly the semi-fast 8.18 a.m. If the M 'R' representative observed those services he would have realised those trains were not affected by cars. In fact, car drivers left their vehicles in the station car parks, continuing their journey by train, limiting the amount of exhaust fumes into the air. An insight into the 'Early B.R. days at Four Oaks' are described in Chapter Two, pp 8-16 in 'Cross City Connections', with eleven illustrations.

The Council offered no objections to the Midland 'Red' service to Coventry, via Walmley, Water Orton, Coleshill and Maxstoke.

OAKHURST, ANCHORAGE ROAD

Owing to a shortage of maternity places in Birmingham, Mary Edwards was transferred to the Oakhurst Nursing Home in Anchorage Road, where Carol Ann was delivered in 1950. In addition to the good standard of care, she thought "it was a lovely place". The grounds were so beautiful and well kept, "people used to come and see the big gardens at the back, and pay a shilling".

Gerry Tayler remembered the "B.B.C. T.V. Transmitter being erected. The B.B.C. have some film taken from the top of it, showing the waving fields of corn as far as the eye could see". A further memory on the borders of Sutton, "was on Blake Street, just by the junction with Clarence Road, stood a shed which sold only one thing, 'Fleur de Lys' pies. We would rush home from the Empress or Odeon to buy a hot pie. In the Winter the owner also sold hot soup".

CURSE OF THE MODERN AGE

Moat House became the new home for Education's Divisional Executive, transferring from St. Nicholas, Upper Clifton Road and the Youth Employment Bureau, probably from Midland Drive. Freres decided the three hundred and sixty pounds well spent on the Town Hall frontage. The weather "had tried its worst to spoil the stonework over the portico. The defective appearance is now a memory". Two public T.V. showings near to the Town Hall and Moat House caught local attention. The Royal Hotel ballroom was crowded by a combined M.W. Lowe and

Mr Barlow's 1950 class at Victoria Road Boys School. - The headmaster,
Mr Gregory on the left, made the author's ears ring on occasions when as a boy
he misbehaved! (Dave Jones/Scholastic Souvenirs Co. Ltd.)

Sutton Coldfield News sponsorship of the 1950 Boat Race, and "200 fans", saw the same sponsors' presentation of the cup Final, in the Lichfield Road Guildhall. Some advocates of family life may have begun to consider that T.V. was "a curse of the modern age", yet another candidate was proposed at BVGS. The speech day speaker, Professor John Morley postulated that the curse, "is regarding work as an ultimate evil". He also decried, according to the News reporter, "early specialisation in any one subject, particularly sciences, a thing to be discouraged".

Sutton Coldfield Hockey side brought some joy into the town by winning the Midland Hockey Festival at Fort Dunlop. Cannock were runners-up and Dunlop third.

LITTLE HOSPITAL EXTRAS

Freres in his weekly columns, reminded readers "it is Sutton Coldfield Hospital", not, "Sutton Coldfield Cottage Hospital", or the "Cottage" as so many prefer to call it. The writer recounted that a resolution was passed at a Governors' Meeting on

June 18th, 1943: Rule one of the constitution was altered to read, "The Institution shall be called Sutton Coldfield Hospital". A T.V. set was handed over to the Hospital by the Mayor as President of the Friends of the Hospital's and Welfare Homes. Councillor H. Hothersall emphasised "we don't do things which the state ought to – we provide those little extras". Similar sets were handed over to the Good Hope Annexe, and to the Home of Rest. The Mayor thanked a number of Societies for donations, including – Emily Broughton Players, Soroptimists and Lady Gardeners Association.

"LITTLE DID WE THINK!"

Immediately after the 1950 Civic Service at the Parish Church, plaques were unveiled in King Edward Square by the newly installed Mayor, Councillor the Revd. H.H. Keyse and dedicated by the Rector, Rev. J.H. Boggon. The Mayor told the crowd, "little did we think when we were gathered at a similar service, thirty years ago, that before another generation had passed we should be recalled to commemorate the names of a further one hundred and ten of those who had fallen in yet another World War". The News itself reported in the June 17th edition, it had "recovered from its Army wounds". Printed on their own rotary press for the

New housing on Falcon Estate including old people's bungalows.
(Birmingham Library Services)

June 24th Issue. It would have larger sized pages – first time in nine years – and it would be completed, editorially and technically by only News personnel. Freres further revealed "that for some time they had wanted to set out, articles, reports, advertisements etc., in a more attractive form".

RESULTS OF RAISING SCHOOL AGE

In the experience of the Sutton Town School Headmistress, Miss S.E. Davies, the outcome of raising the school leaving age from fourteen to fifteen years of age, though opposed by some, "had in the main been successful". However, the "lack of buildings and staff shortages, made it chaotic in the early stages". The advantages she had witnessed were "taking of more responsibility, and a more balanced judgement", with the young person, "taking a greater initiative". Although some, "would have been better off earning a living, most found it to their benefit".

Within the additional year she considered the school's chief aim should be "a) to teach children how to live together, b) the need to educate them to contribute to general good of the world, c) make most of leisure, so that greed, self-seeking might be lessened if not banished completely, d) harmony needed first in living with the family, then school, later to the nation. Good relations", she argued "leads to international goodwill". The Headmistress concluded in her lecture to the Sutton Soroptimists "we try to link the fourth senior year with life as it will be after the child leaves school".

Members from a Sutton area church wished they had never gone to a North West holiday resort. Six members of the Banners Gate Congregational Church ended up in a Blackpool Hospital. According to the News reporter they were suffering from food poisoning contracted at one of Blackpool's many guest houses.

SUTTON COLLEGE OF ART EXHIBITION

The small, "but fully recognised Sutton Coldfield School of Art, offered full and part-time study in all phases of Art". The advantages of the local College included a) time saved in travelling and b) in expenditure. In the 1949-50 year there were three hundred and one full-time, part-time and evening students. The exhibition displayed the variety of talents realised by the different courses on show in Sutton Library. A cement shortage held up local schemes, due partly to the growing use of concrete. Priorities were to Gas and Electric Boards, Atomic Research stations and other indirect Government Departments. The next selection of Falcon Lodge Estate Road names were St. Chads Road, Horsfall Road, Colmore Drive and Glover Road. Sadler Road off Linridge Road was also released.

A 1950 scene of Fowler Road. (Birmingham Library Services)

SUTTON – CYCLISTS' PARADISE

"Cycle Dodger", in the Readers' Letters, vigorously complained how in 1950 cyclists were causing havoc by pushing their "cycles in one's back", particularly in the Parade area. "They had no regard for people's clothes or limbs". C.D. concluded that, "in no other town have I seen cycles wheeled around on the pavement to this extent and I cannot imagine why it is allowed in Sutton Coldfield!" In the same issue it was reported a cyclist who failed to keep left when riding a pedal cycle from Mill Street was fined five shillings by Sutton Magistrates.

THURSDAY CRICKET LEAGUE

A Sutton Mayor referred to the Thursday afternoon half-closing habits of Suttonians. David Jones brought to mind how some Sutton shop staff used the free Thursday afternoons in the Summer. His father, Wilf Jones, was the Vice-Captain

The Sutton Thursday Cricket team played their home games in Rectory Park.
(David Jones)

of the Sutton Thursday Cricket side. Home games were played in Rectory Park. David's brothers Peter and Graham are shown with their father, dressed in the Club's Cricket blazer, second front left, is Bill Petty, Bakery supervisor. Second from left on the back row, is Bill Price, a Prudential Insurance Agent, whose day off was Thursday. "He was the regular Captain and Wicket-keeper, and good friend of the family". Bill's wife Al, helped David's mother with the teas. "Mother would take cakes and sandwiches from the Bakery to help out. Father was a middle order batsman and a fast bowler with a twenty yard run". David recalled there was, "a real team spirit amongst the Thursday team, and if Captain Bill was not available, father would act as Vice-Captain". They played teams from Aldridge, Walsall and Wolverhampton.

SUTTON COLDFIELD C.C. 'A' XI

Wilf Jones was also involved with the Sutton Coldfield C.C. 'A' XI, which he was in charge of. When the Sunday second XI were short, he would step in to help. Mr Jones at times used some of the young lads from Bishop Vesey's School in the Saturday afternoon team, giving them the opportunity to play against adults. Regrettably, Wilf had to retire from Cricket in "the early 1950's, as he lost the sight of one eye when a starting handle came out of one of the old cars and damaged his eye. He later took up golf and joined Moor Hall G.C. and was very successful at the game". In a sponsored six rounds in a day, from 3.45 a.m. – 9 p.m., he raised £500 for a local charity.

SUTTON COLDFIELD, BIRMINGHAM!

There was much heated debate in the Sutton Council Chamber because the Post Office decided to change the Royal Town's postal address to Sutton Coldfield, Birmingham. The Town Clerk was told to pursue the matter urgently. Councillor H. Hothersall believed it should be "Sutton Coldfield, Warwickshire", he added, "the Town is becoming well-known, especially since the opening of the T.V. Station". The Councillor, "did not think it necessary to add the name of a neighbouring town".

Apparently the Wesleyan Hall in South Parade had to be completely modernised after its use as the British Restaurant. The "acoustic difficulties have been overcome by boarding-in portions of the ceiling and treating the walls with a special paint". The stage was considered to be one of the best in the town, providing "something of the atmosphere of a little theatre".

PENNS TO CLOSE?

There were anxieties expressed in Walmley of rumours over the closure of Penns Station. Having received representations from Walmley residents, Sir John Mellor took the concerns to Lord Hurcomb, Chairman of the British Transport Commission. Lord Hurcomb advised the Sutton M.P., "it is not proposed to close this station at the present time, and the buildings have in fact, recently been repaired and re-painted". Such railway talk was often construed by railway employees as the prelude to closure!

The U.K. weather caused a serious water shortage in Sutton in June and an appeal two months later by local farmers "for a fortnight's fine weather to get their crops safely in".

Penns Station showing the Birmingham side platform. (Les Hollins)

The Midland 'Red', in liaison with the Town Council moved the loading point for 105, S65 and S72 services, which all went through Walmley from Victoria Road to South Parade, vehicles returning to South Parade via Victoria Road. All journeys in the Tamworth direction were to load from the shelter at the bottom of Mill Street and Trinity Hill, instead of the 'Roses' end of the Parade.

Sutton Coldfield's own Ronnie Hancock and his band completed a successful Summer season at a Hotel in Torquay, Devon. Patrons appreciated the entertainment so much the Manager extended the Band's contract into early September.

T.V. MAST DESIGNER'S SURPRISE

Sutton Coldfield Rotary Club members suffered with optical illusions during an official visit ten months after the B.B.C. T.V. Transmitter had opened. A report noted, "Standing at the base of the huge towering 750 foot mast and looking up at the passing clouds, it gives the impression that it is moving". The party were advised the designer anticipated the "One hundred and forty ton structure would move". Similar to Mr Green's description, the Club members saw, "a colossal amount of apparatus and complicated machinery which brings the pictures" to the T.V. sets.

CLARENCE ROAD VIEW OF T.V. MAST

Derek Sutton remembers the view of the Sutton Coldfield T.V. Mast from the Clarence Road family home. His deceased father, Jim, took the picture of the Mast, with "The Old Farm", owned by a Mr Nicholls, in the foreground. The farmer "had pigs, which he sometimes butchered on the farm, two horses and potatoes on his land, which stretched to the railway line". As well as the farm, Mr Nicholls had a smithy in Tennant Street, Birmingham, where he shod his own 'Old Farm' horses". Mr Nicholls had two sons. Recalling later history of the farm, Derek wrote "the farm was eventually sold to two elderly spinster ladies, one was said to have been a nurse in France during the First World War. When they sold up, Weymouth Drive and some houses were built on the land".

Clarence Road view of the T.V. masts. (Jim Sutton)

HILL INFANTS' SCHOOL

There was a market garden on the other side of the railway, owned by Mr Jack Badger. "His wife taught at Hill Infants' School in Mere Green Road. This building still exists as a youth centre. She went on to teach in Hill Boys' School, the land of which later became a supermarket car park". Derek Sutton, "attended both of these schools, and had to walk from Clarence Road, as there were no buses along the road to where we lived". Mr Sutton's V.J. Day Celebration party photograph in 1945, was taken in the field behind "the Clarence Road houses, which has since been built on".

The 1945 VJ Day Celebrations party held in the field behind the Clarence Road houses. (D. Sutton)

WHAT'S UNDER STREETLY?

An earlier account in the News about boring for coal seams under Streetly brought a statement from the boring company's Managing Director, Mr W. Price. He "assured the S.C.N. that the test boring was to confirm geologists' theories that the coal seam extends under Streetly and that if it does, it will be mined from Hamstead Colliery". There still remained some concern in the village "that the coal seam could affect land and property above". The coal seams were estimated to be almost "two thousand feet below ground". Some villagers wondered if further development in the locality would be affected. Mr Price was adamant, "the plan for building one thousand, two hundred and thirty houses, sixteen shops and a cinema, will not in the least be prejudiced": the boring was expected to continue into the New Year.

SUTTON'S LOSS TO LONDON

One of Pat Collins most popular rides at the Crystal Palace site was to be moved to the 1951 Great Festival of Britain venue on the Thames Embankment. Many West Midland patrons regretted the loss of such a prestige ride. Nothing else, it was claimed could replace the Big Dipper.

Pedestrians adjusting to road works at the Empress end of South Parade in 1950. (Bernard R. Haynes)

ANGRY HOUSEWIVES

A past President of the Birmingham District Butchers' and Pork Butchers' Trade and Benevolent Association faced a tirade of angry and distraught Sutton housewives. Why, the guest speaker was persistently asked "were cattle being killed whilst in a distressed condition"? They further wanted to know from the expert "why the carcasses were given no time to 'condition' – a process which made meat more tender?" It was explained that in "pre-control days butchers were 'meat proud' and 'shop proud', often killing their own animals, after they had rested them, allowing the meat to be conditioned before offering it for sale". In the Post-War ration days "Butchers had a permit to the value of meat sufficient for the needs of his rationed customers and what kind of meat it was, tough or tender, was purely a matter of luck". The speaker tried to placate the restless audience by reminding them, "the butcher himself had 'no say' in the matter". Presumably the Sutton housewives advocating the return of pre-War service would have welcomed Hill Village's own shop, that closed in the War, re-opening after six years. Some villagers "had bought their goods at the store for more than thirty years". Shoppers were forced to go down to Mere Green. Thanks to Mr and Mrs H.S. Jenkins, Hill Villagers were saved a half-mile journey, plus "a bigger variety of goods".

Mrs Crockett at the Ebrook Road shop, lost her husband in 1950, and this left a large responsibility on her shoulders as she tried to run the local shop on her own.

RILAND BEDFORD SECONDARY SCHOOL

The much postponed Pre-War built school, used by the American Forces from 1942-1945, had its first assembly of staff and children.

The News noted "Hill and Town Girls' primary schools transferred to the new Secondary School on October 3rd". The Ministry of Education authorised provision of "permanent offices to replace temporary arrangements made by the adaptation of science room in the boys' wing for about seven thousand, one hundred and forty pounds". The boys arrived in 1951.

The Borough Libraries in the 1949-50 years had fourteen thousand, five hundred and thirty-two registered readers, thirty-one per cent of the population. There was a national decline in book borrowing, the largest local decrease was at Boldmere. The Hospital service had been well used. The decline according to the Libraries Annual Report, "cannot be attributed to the extension of T.V. in the Midlands". T. Barratt and Co Ltd, Mill Street, offered a rented Pye Black Screen T.V. at eight and ninepence per week (on average). The service included free replacement of Cathode Ray tubes, valves and components.

SERVING A ROYAL

An item of November 11th explained that as the Princess Royal was in mourning over the death of King Gustav of Sweden, H.R.H. wore black, when accepting purses for the Y.M.C.A .War and National Service Fund. She was delighted that the local Sutton target of fifteen hundred pounds had been passed by four hundred and thirty-three pounds, she received the donations on a decorated stage, at the Town Hall, which had recently been renovated. A personal insight into H.R.H. family life, probably touched a chord in many parents at the gift day. In replying to the Civic, welcome, she shared "many mothers must be grateful for the work of the Y.M.C.A. during the War. I would like to tell you that both my sons, when they first joined the Army, were deeply grateful for what the Y.M.C.A. did for them". I wonder if the waitress who served H.R.H., Mrs M. Salter of Ebrook Road was the mother of potential theatre manager Jeff Salter, of Tom Sawyer fame? Summing up the occasion Mrs Salter said, "it was a very thrilling and very wonderful day. It is not very often we get a Royal visitor to Sutton, and the opportunity of serving a Princess, comes once in a lifetime".

Development of Falcon Lodge Estate with the former Barrage Balloon Depot in the background. (Birmingham Library Services)

NEW GROUPS

Tudor cycling group, recently formed by a group of local enthusiasts, were already promoting three races in 1951, all over the fourteen-and-a-quarter mile circuit of Roughley-Lichfield-Mere Green-Roughley, beginning with the Junior Road Race Championship (South Midland Section) in June, covering fifty-seven miles in four laps. The August fixture was the hundred miles Amateur Grand Prix for all senior amateurs. The third Tudor Cycling Club event was in September for second and third-class seniors, racing over eighty-six miles in six laps. A further new organisation was the Sutton Park Protection Association formed at a public meeting at St. Peter's Hall, Maney. It was decided that the Association would work with the Council, though acting firmly when the amenities of the Park were endangered. Mr K.C. Blacklock was elected Chairman and seventeen other officers appointed.

A new organ was dedicated at Holy Trinity Church, replacing one that had seen service for fifty years. The special nature of the service commemorated the six hundred and fifty years anniversary of the Church.

John Platt's four 'Top of the Pops for 1950' were 'Music, Music, Music', 'Mona Lisa', 'Be My Love', and the 'Tennessee Waltz'.

WHEATMOORE INVENTIONS

This synopsis of local farmer, John Gilmour's 'seventy years Heritage 1928 to 1998', provides further observations around Sutton Coldfield of farming, confirming and developing views shared by two other farmers already considered. Within Mr Gilmour's twenty page A4 size document, readers learn of the many farming inventions of his late Father, Mr James Gilmour, John's own, and the production of Wheatmoore farm prototypes, by Rubery Owen and other well and lesser-known companies. John's source document outlines some of the Heritage pursuits followed by Wheatmoore Farm, and gives in depth data of the machines and equipment associated with the local farm through seventy years.

GREAT DEPRESSION

Thirty-nine year old Ayrshire farmer, James Gilmour, arrived at Wheatmoore Farm, Tamworth Road, Sutton Coldfield in 1928, taking on the tenancy in 1929. It was the time of the Great Depression. Wheatmoore's two previous tenants found it impossible to keep the farm viable. Some landlords, keen to have their farms running, took no rent from the tenants for the first three years, on the understanding that the tenants would stay after the initial period. Tenant farmers on the heavy soils were most at risk. Wise and canny Mr Gilmour selected Wheatmoore Farm near the Whitehouse Common Cross-Roads with its close proximity to Birmingham markets and Sutton Coldfield. From the ordinary mixed farm with its main products of potatoes and milk, he quickly made use of the quite substantial, at least in those days, milking herd of around thirty-five cows. He delivered fresh milk by pony and float before breakfast, seven days a week, to Sutton Coldfield customers who were impressed by his business acumen. They were further ready to acknowledge the farmer's dedication to quality service by his heavy investment into installing electricity throughout the farm, enabling milking by hand to be replaced with a powered milking process.

James Gilmour, an innovative Scottish Farmer, arrived in Sutton between the war years.
(John Gilmour Collection)

The slick presentation of the potatoes, learned in Ayrshire, having been riddled, graded and weighed before sale to the growing number of Merchants with motor lorries, brought Mr Gilmour senior, compliments and many repeat orders. A "large part of the potato crop was consumed fairly locally." He supplied local greengrocers, roundsmen and stores, backing up the trade to the Birmingham Vegetable market conveyed there by the motor lorry Merchants. The Ayrshire Man's various systems were "very much ahead of their time".

NOTABLE TRANSACTIONS

As business grew Mrs Isabella Gilmour took a more prominent part in the marketing with the five or six regular potato merchants. A fascinating glimpse of trading transactions in between the two World Wars was shown by Mr Henley. When he bought a product from Mrs Gilmour he simply wrote on an ordinary piece of paper the agreed amount he owed for say, the potatoes and signed it. Every time it was honoured by the Bank. He never owned a cheque book. Another innovation in Warwickshire was Jame's Bag Muck, or Artificial Fertiliser. Supplies from Patullo Higgs, of Orpington, arrived at Four Oaks Goods Siding by the L.M.S., usually in sixteen, ten or eight stone hessian sacks. The Gilmours or staff collected the consignment by tractor and trailer. Deliveries later transferred to road transport, direct to Wheatmoore. In his paper, John disclosed that the main Fertiliser elements were: Sulphate of Ammonia Crystals, Power Super Phosphates, Muirlate, and Sulphate of Potash, mixed together in different proportions. Richard Lewis, employed at the farm before the Scottish invasion of 1928, always assisted in the mixing processes, He worked on the farm for over forty years and lived until he was ninety-seven. In the early nineteen thirties the young lads on the farm, like John, manned a machine that made a fizzing noise as the compressed air was released while being lowered. The machine was a useful implement planting four hundred acres of potatoes annually throughout W.W.II. It was later completely restored.

Mrs Isabella Gilmour introduced additional marketing skills as the business grew. (John Gilmour Collection, J.S.D. Kirkman)

PNEUMATIC TYRES ON AGRICULTURAL EQUIPMENT

Mr James Gilmour's realisation of the considerable use that could be made of pneumatic tyres on agricultural equipment was laughed at by the Dunlop Tyre Company Departments he approached. Mr Gilmour tested a pair of old aircraft wheels and tyres on a horse cart used around Wheatmoore Farm, finding them to be far superior to alternatives. Eventually Dunlop's Chairman, Sir Eric Geddis, had two pairs of rear tyres made for an agricultural tractor. The Company showed their disbelief in the Chairman's faith in the Gilmour's by charging the two tyres to Sir Eric's personal account! The effectiveness of the pneumatic tyres was borne out when all the Wheatmoore Farm wheeled machines and implements were fitted with the superior tyres. Presumably many Dunlop Heads of Departments apologised to their Chairman.

GILMOUR EXPANSION

The Agricultural Ministry's directive to utilise all unused land to produce food in W.W.II, encouraged James Gilmour to weed out a considerable number of plots. Before the end of the War he was paying rent to twenty-two Landlords. His tractors with special low-slung chassis trailers became a common sight around the North side of Sutton. For example, the previously hidden wasting away acres included: a) two fields amounting to fourteen acres behind the Mere Green factory of Lucas; b) part of Moor Hall Golf Club; c) and a six acre field with a school built on it by the owner, who taught in the school. John Gilmour recounts "the major factor that made it possible for us to cultivate these parcels of land that were dotted around the outskirts of the town, was the use of pneumatic tyres". Such countrywide direct contributions to land utilisation, greatly assisted the British food shortage.

ALLURING FACTORY WAGES

Another nineteen thirties development was the hedge-cutting machine. The eventual successful mid-mounted position was arrived at by the modification of the old haysweep framework with some engineering and structural changes by Charles James Daws at the Four Oaks Forge. The Gilmours witnessed many skilled farm workers attracted away by city factories "for higher wages and less weather-prone conditions". As one of our farmers contributed earlier, such poaching of agricultural workers and farm mechanisation, saw many countryside trades go into serious decline.

POTATO GANGS

In the Post-War years Wheatmoore Farm was still used as a testing centre for James Gilmour's inventions and ideas from manufacturers. One company's engineer had a caravan with his family on the farm whilst he carried out tests on equipment over nearly two years. Gangs of helpers were transported by Wheatmoore Farm, particularly for potato picking. John said "some of the gangs could be fifty or more strong, and as many as three gangs working at one time". A Morris Commercial ex-Military Signals Van, was fitted with a drawbar to tow an adapted four-wheel flat-bed trailer with a canvas

Potato Planting - W.W.II - at Wheatmoor Farm, Tamworth Road. The horse is with Percy Lines, while the women planters are nearer to Walter Hobday on the tractor and covering implement. (J. Gilmour Collection)

weather protection cover. "This outfit was used very successfully for many years, going regularly to Mile Oak, Tamworth and Amington to collect or return the many faithful workers".

Mr Gilmour's paper includes details of the first Combine at Wheatmoore, a Minneapolis Moline trailer machine, British built under licence, and some heavy plant equipment for various tasks at the many Gilmour locations.

FORTIES – NINETEEN-FIFTY:

From pre-World War II, through the War and into peacetime, this volume has shared many stories, some told for the first time, of life experienced by people in and around Sutton Coldfield, from different backgrounds. In addition to the on-the-spot human pictures, they are supplemented by a number of unnamed Sutton Coldfield News Reporters, like other contributors, bringing something of themselves, values and human tendencies to the jigsaw picture of 1930-1950 in Sutton Coldfield from many perspectives.

THE STORY TO COME – THE FIFTIES:

Rather surprisingly for some readers, rationing continued on into the fifties, the population also continues to grow in Sutton Coldfield. Increasing N.H.S. provision is clamoured for, The Town is traumatised by seventeen fatalities and many injured in the 1955 train crash. Steam trains lose out to diesel multiple units in 1956, which brought a record passenger take-up.

The Town from 1954/6 was taken up with preparing for the World Jamboree in 1957, which was disrupted by planned vandalism a few months before the opening. The end of 1959 was reached with many Post-War achievements like the model Falcon Lodge Estate, emerging to maturity, but other essential needs still being unfulfilled. 1951-1959 are documented by local folk, service staff at R.A.F. 216 M.U., and the mainly unnamed professional journalists of the Sutton Coldfield News.

The S.M.R. closed at the end of the 1962 Pat Collins season, when the ground lease for the Crystal Palace area ran out. The May 2002 picture shows the resurrection of "Sutton Flyer" with the SMR railcar in the background.

From right to left at New Romney are George Barlow B.E.M., veteran Romney Hythe and Dymchurch driver and engineer, John Tidmarsh, John Ward and Bill Hunt, all ex-S.M.R.

An up-date of the S.M.R. and its new life in Lincolnshire appears in 'Sutton Coldfield In The Fifties'.

Suttonian John Hicks captures some of the 1955 train crash scene. (John Hicks)

Resurrection of 'Sutton Flyer' with the SMR railcar in the background, 2002. (John Tidmarsh)

A birdseye view of a Sutton location in the mid 1950's, showing an area in the north of the town. (BVGS, Aerofilms)

PREVIOUS BOOKS BY THE AUTHOR

Cross City Connections: Brewin Books, 1990

This remains the book with the most data and pictures of the stations and railway lines in the Borough of Sutton Coldfield 1940-1990. A considerable number of contributors were railway personnel, and some of their contributions have now been 'borrowed', without permission, by later authors!

Wheels Around Sutton, Lichfield and Tamworth: Brewin Books, 1997

Against the background of the wider Midland 'Red', this book traces the living history of public transport in Sutton Coldfield 1913-1973, the emergence of A.T. Hastilow's 'Tudor Rose' Coaches, and Harper Bros of Heath Hayes. With previously unpublished material by staff and customers at Sutton Coldfield, Lichfield and Tamworth, this book provides new perspectives of public transport in these areas.

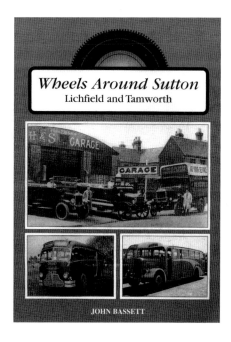

ABOUT THE AUTHOR

John Bassett was born, educated and lived in Sutton Coldfield from 1935 - 1963. His employment on British Railways 1950-53 and 1955-57 is covered in 'Cross City Connections.' In later years John qualified as a Field Social Worker, Further Education Teacher and Training Officer.

In 1984 he became a full time Railway Chaplain with the Railway Mission, becoming responsible in 1985 for the West Midlands, operating from Birmingham New Street Station.

After completing part-time courses at Northern College, Manchester and the University of Manchester over four years, John was ordained as a Non-Stipendiary Minister with the United Reformed Church in 1993. He was inducted on New Street Station with the encouragement and support of Railway management and staff.

At the request of Sir Richard Branson, the Rev John Bassett officiated at the renewal of marriage vows and promises by a Virgin Train Manager and his wife during a scheduled Wolverhampton to London Euston service. The couple celebrated their 25th Wedding Anniversary and the Train Manager's 25 years on the railways. The Rev Bassett retired in 2000, with some of his time now being used to research his new series on Sutton Coldfield. He now lives in Lichfield.

(Photograph courtesy of Virgin Trains)